Belief Systems

(& *other* b.s.)

by Angus W. Stocking, L.S

Dear Art,
May this book
mark a new epoch
in your life!
Cheers,

AntStg

1st Edition

BLB

Boundary Line Books
Paonia, Colorado

Belief Systems (& Other B.S.)
by Angus W. Stocking, L.S.

1st Edition
ISBN 0-9765043-1-6

Published by Boundary Line Books
SAN256-386X
P.O. Box 695
Paonia CO 81428
970.527.4923
970.527.4843 fax
boundarylinebooks.com

Table of Contents
dedication, acknowledgements, introduction

colophon

Dedication

This book is dedicated to KVNF Community Radio and the staff, volunteers, and listeners who make it the best radio station of any size, anywhere.

Acknowledgements

The writings of Robert Anton Wilson have influenced my life profoundly, and the essays contained herein. This book would not exist if it had not been a radio show first, and the radio show would not exist if KVNF Station Manager Sally Kane had not invited me - when we were first introduced! - to be 'a local Andrei Codrescu'... while I haven't been *that*, Sally has always been amazingly supportive. Likewise, Skip Naft has produced the show from the beginning and contributed substantially to the sound and content - in particular, he has often goaded me to write snappier endings. The Town of Paonia and all of KVNF's listeners have been a very kind and perceptive audience and a pleasure to write for. In the year I have lived in the Western Slope I have been befriended by so many positive, loving people that I can't list them by name, but let me at least shout out to the Blue Sage, Pizza My Heart, The Old River Road Trading Post, Nelle's, Moonrise Espresso, the Paradise Theatre and... jeez, there's even too many *institutions* to single out; it's a great place to live. I am grateful to Christopher Dougherty for printing this book and for many interesting conversations - and also for his friendship. My mother, Corinth Stocking, is everything a son could ask for. My wife, Lisa Cassle, is an ardent supporter and fierce partisan. Finally, Lisa and I both gratefully acknowledge the blessings of our patron goddess, Ostara.

Introduction

"Belief is the death of intelligence" - Robert Anton Wilson

"The one place gods indubitably exist is in human minds." - Alan Moore

The quotations above have served as my touchstones for several years. I came across them when I was still a zealous, true believing member of a fundamentalist Christian cult. They were the perfect little mental bon-bon, just tempting enough to retain and savor, just unassuming enough to not obviously threaten the beliefs I was so assiduously cultivating. But they were also seeds, perhaps *the* seeds, that eventually led me to change my life radically.

Wilson's point is devilishly simple; the moment we profess 'belief', we begin to limit our ability to evaluate new evidence. That is, by 'accepting' a belief, we relieve ourselves of the responsibility to *re*evaluate as needed - our thinking becomes rigid. In my case, accepting and then preaching a complex, precise dogma had made me into something of a spiritual automaton; I was prodigiously good at bending every thought - every *thought* - to the service of the dogma and had nearly lost the ability to simply observe and respond.

Wilson also teaches that we all live in 'reality tunnels'; sets of beliefs that shape and limit what we are able to perceive and, thus, the world that we are able to live in. By systematically examining and surpassing our assumptions about reality, we can experience bigger, more enjoyable realities. If we are to believe Wilson, *we* are the 'Master Who Makes the Green Grass Green'.

Something in me cracked a little when I read this. A little light came in. Though I spent years extending the insight, even then I could almost see that *my* beliefs were limiting. In the first paragraph, I used the word 'cultivating' to describe my attitude toward belief, and that's exactly what I was doing. I *had* the belief, and I was doing everything I could to *maintain* it - *rather than changing my beliefs to accommodate new experiences and new learning.*

Moore's observation is also rather simple. He wisely avoids the question of whether gods have any *objective* existence - after millennia, all we can really do is shrug this question off. He simply insists on the irrefutable fact that they *certainly* exist as mental constructs. And this leads to all sorts of delightful - or distressing, depending on your circumstances - speculation about just who is being served: a god, or a *conception* of a god?

The idea extends nicely to constructs like governments, philosophies and corporations; what, really, are we being loyal *to*?

The two together add up to a personal philosophy. Strive relentlessly for *awareness* of one's own set of beliefs in order to transcend them, and more than that, be *wary* of widely held beliefs. I am happy to say that my own experiments with this basic philosophy have been extremely positive and that I have had more love, joy, and prosperity in my life as a result.

If there is a theme weaving through this book, it is that in every essay I am trying to help others to examine and transcend *their* belief systems and, maybe, be a little happier as a result.

Cheers,
Angus W. Stocking
Paonia, CO 2005

Of everything I've written, the following piece has generated by far the most response. I'm glad. It's one of those stories that took a couple of years to write, as different puzzle parts fell into place. There were a couple of things I didn't try to include in the published article (which first appeared in a magazine for land surveyors) or the radio show. For one, it was really odd how information came to me about this. For example, the occult book mentioned (it is alarmingly titled, Conjuring Spirits) practically jumped out at me from a bookstore shelf and opened in my hands to the Kaballah square that began to tie everything together. Another, weirder, happenstance had to do with my study of a classic 'master' conspiracy theory known as the Sirius Mystery, and centering on a book of that title by Robert Temple, and also on an underground bestseller by über conspiracy theorist Robert Anton Wilson titled Cosmic Trigger. The basic idea of the Sirius Mystery is that beings from the Sirius star system visited several ancient civilizations to jumpstart human technology, while also providing the magickal basis for every conspiracy since, from the Knights Templar to the Priory of Sion (don't ask). Naturally, they are in psychic contact with some humans, and intend to return fairly soon...

Anyway, Wilson's book mentioned that he and two other writers, Doris Lessing and Phillip K. Dick, all wrote books about aliens from Sirius at more or less the same time, and without having any contact each other. I'd read Dick's book, and decided to read Lessing's, Shikasta. It's a good read, but most notable for me was one of the book's concluding passages, which described **the gridded look of the sectionalized United States and attributed it to the evil 'Shikasta' influence!** *It was an odd moment; two separate conspiracy type thingies that I had been studying and thinking and talking about obsessively for more than a year suddenly and unexpectedly came together with a bang. For a couple of days, the world was a different place for me.*

I've been asked if I 'believe' in the sectional conspiracy. I'm not sure how to answer. I certainly believe in the facts presented. Do I believe that a secretive group cast a Kabbalistic magick spell over the developing Unites States? Or do I think, rather, that I have just found a clever way to map odd information onto an exceedingly complicated topic. I don't know. And I can't figure out what the difference is between the two possibilities.

Sectional Strangeness

ne of the problems with *not* being a conspiracy theorist is that one has no easy explanations when faced with some of the more glaring oddities of the world around us. It is, for example, passing strange that the dollar bill features an all-seeing eye and pyramid and the fact that it *can* be explained does not mean that it *has* been explained, if you follow my drift. Similarly, the non-conspiracy theorist is forced into some fancy mental gymnastics when considering glaringly obvious phenomena, such as the presence of two Skull-and-Bonesmen in the 2004 presidential election, the screwy layout of Washington D.C., and the pentagonal shape of the world's most powerful military headquarters. Mundane explanations exist for all of these, but since they are bizarre facts to begin with, the mind is more comfortable with bizarre explanations involving the Illuminati, aliens, or the occult.

My own personal example of this began one morning when I was considering the Public Lands Survey System (PLSS) township layout, the 6x6 boustrephedonic square made up of 36 square mile 'sections'. 'Boustrephedonic', incidentally, is the word for the right-to-left, left-to-right layout of the square – it's from the Greek, and means 'as an ox plows' and in this case describes the descending, switchbacking layout of the square - see the illustration. I've always wondered about the township layout; why, for instance, is it boustrephedonic, and why is it 6x6, and not some other number? Idly, I added up the columns and rows, to see if there were any 'magic square' properties in the design. The columns all add up to 111 – try it yourself. A little experimentation showed that this is a feature of boustrephedonic squares with even, but not odd, numbered sides, so this is not mysterious. The rows, on the other hand, seemed to yield no pattern of interest... until I took one more step. I 'reduced' the numbers numerologically to yield a single digit number. That is, I added together the digits of the multi-digit numbers, and if the result was multi-digit I added again until a one digit number resulted. As seen below, the numerological sum of all the rows is three, and it takes no special flash of insight to see that the numerological sum of 111, the column sum, is *also* three. Curious.

6	5	4	3	2	1	$1+2+3+4+5+6 = 21, 2+1 = 3$
7	8	9	10	11	12	$= 57, 5+7 = 12, 1+2 = 3$
18	17	16	15	14	13	$= 93, 9+3 = 12, 1+2 = 3$
19	20	21	22	23	24	$= 129, 1+2+9 = 12, 1+2 = 3$
30	29	28	27	26	25	$= 165, 1+6+5 = 12, 1+2 = 3$
31	32	33	34	35	36	$= 201, 2+0+1 = 3$

All columns add up to 111, $1+1+1 = 3$

I should say, here, that I am not much of a numerologist. I don't work out year numbers, or look for numerological significance in the dates of my life. Still, I did read a book about it once, and took away numerological reduction as a sort of 'mental fidgeting'. And number mysticism has a history in the West that goes all the way back to Pythagoras and his followers. Many great minds have succumbed, and the results are not always pretty. Isaac Newton, for example, spent at least as much time on numerical Biblical exegesis as he did on scientific work and his writings on those topics strike modern readers as deranged. Two modern movies, *Pi* and *A Beautiful Mind* explore the tendency of the mind to project numerological meaning onto complex phenomena.

Be that as it may and ignoring, for the moment, the possibility that *I* was succumbing to number mysticism, the undeniable fact remained that the GLO township is a numerological magic square. I worked out boustrephedonic squares from 2x2 to 9x9, and *only* the 6x6 square has this property.

So; now what? Well, not having all that many facts at hand, I immediately began to theorize. Eventually, I came up with rather an elaborate scenario involving Thomas Jefferson, the Illuminati, and aerial photography – it was good for at least 20 minutes of happy hour conversation. But, upon investigation, the hypothesis broke down. Jefferson, for example, preferred a 10x10 square and there is no evidence of Illuminati involvement... but then, there wouldn't be, would there? So I began to tire of the whole thing; not that I disbelieved my nutty theory, necessarily, but I began to bore even myself.

Kaballah?

Two actual facts got me interested again. First, when reading a book about the Jewish system of mysticism known as Kaballah (or Cabala, or Qaballah, or any of several variants – take your pick) I happened across the following figure.

6	32	3	34	35	1
7	11	27	28	8	30
19	14	16	15	23	24
18	20	22	21	17	13
25	29	10	9	26	12
36	5	33	4	2	31

Kaballah magic square - every row and column adds up to 111, which reduces numerologically to 3. Since the 6th sephiroth of the Kaballistic Tree of Life is associated with the Sun, this 6x6 square is also associated with the Sun.

It turns out that conventional magic squares are important in Kaballah, and are associated with the planets and astrological magic. The 6x6 square is associated with the sun, and is therefore the most powerful of these. One text of Western Occultism (for which Kaballah is a major source), dating from the 1400s, says of it, "The figure of the Sun is appropriated for kings and princes of this world, and it is square and has a grid of six, and it is the figure of *total power.*"

Now, I only sort of believe in astrological magic, or rather, I'm learning to suspend judgement about the exotic belief systems of others, but it is a fact that humans have apparently *always* used the progressions of the night sky for mystical purposes, and after 1,000's of years, astrology very much remains part of our world – something about it is irresistibly seductive to some human minds. And interestingly, amazing feats of engineering have a long association with astronomy and astrology. The Pyramids, of course, and Stonehenge, are just two of the many examples of major ancient accomplishments which are now believed to have been largely motivated by astrological concerns. But considered as a whole, the township system is this planet's most significant man made feature – it would swallow thousands of Great Walls. It is easily visible from space. Which leads to the rather strange thought that future archaeologists, investigating the wonder that was America, will uncover the whole system of townships and naturally conclude that early Americans were determined to stamp the 'figure of the Sun' across the entire Continent – and nearly succeeded.

An Apocalyptic Sum

I'll admit, I could have done without the second actual fact that got me interested again in township oddities. Late in 2003, after I had been musing about these things for a couple of years, I was looking again at a township layout (they were, after all, a major feature of my job) and suddenly wondered what the numbers 1 through 36 add up to. That is, what is the sum of the 36 township squares? I've learned since that there's an easy way to sum up long series of numbers, but I didn't know it at the time so I just took out my trusty Hewlett Packard and cranked out an answer. Then, hoping I'd made a mistake, I added them up again... and then I did it one more time just to be sure. The sum is - and some of you are probably way ahead of me here – 666, also known as "The Number of the Beast".

> *Here is the key; and anyone who has intelligence may work out the number of the beast. The number represents a man's name, and the numerical value of its letters is six hundred and sixty-six.* – Revelation 13:18, New English Bible

Now What?

To sum up then, the GLO township is a unique numerological magic square, very similar to squares associated with Kaballah and used in Western Occultism for hundreds of years. In a major feat of engineering, it has been stamped across much of the United States. The sum of its individual squares is 666, a number of apocalyptic significance to many.

Now what is the poor non-conspiracy theorist to do, faced with such a rich source of peculiarity? Probably the best thing to do is to ignore such rabbit holes, but instead I began to wonder about possible motivations. That is, if there *were* some shadowy group behind all this, what might their motives have been?

Because the GLO square has definitely had a major effect on the United States, quite aside from its impact on surveying. Fly over the United States, or look at aerial photos. You will see a grid, a chessboard; square fields or developed blocks bounded by straight roads. No other sector of the Earth is laid out like this. Fly over any part of Europe, or Asia, or South America, or… anywhere but here, really. You will see roads and fields that follow contours, that give way to hills and mountains, that nestle up to forest edges and creeks. You will see a human landscape that is *shaped by* the natural world; but in the United States, most of us live in a landscape that is *imposed upon* the natural world, laid over it like graph paper on a map. The township system is part of the structural underpinning of U.S. culture, part of every American's mental furniture. It may not be, quite, the air we breathe but it is certainly the ground we walk on. It shapes our visible world and it shapes us.

Is it too crazy, too speculative, to say that Americans are a different people as a result of our different environment, that our national culture is partially a product of our national landscape? As a nation, we do tend to ride roughshod, at times, over the natural world. Could our straight roads and square fields be shaping us as much as we shape them?

Now here I speculate wildly, but bear with me. One word for the tendency to impose order on nature is 'Apollonian'. The sun god, Apollo, has long been associated with classical order, control, discipline and masculinity – as opposed to the Moon Goddess, traditionally associated with wildness, paganism, and femininity. As a nation, the United States is considerably more 'solar' than 'lunar'.

But since the 6x6 square is a solar device, a fascinating (and, yes, nutty and conspiratorial) possibility comes to mind. There is the interesting, unlikely, crazy possibility that some person or group manipulated the choice of GLO township layout in an attempt to cast a Kabbalistic spell over an entire nation… and there is the possibility that it worked.

Tarot Temptations

The fundamentalist Christian cult to which I belonged for 17 years had a special horror of divination in general and of Tarot in particular. Tarot cards were declared unequivocally to be Satanic and the cult's dreary magazines used Tarot images as a sort of graphic shorthand for all that is demonic and perverse. So naturally, when I began to deprogram myself, Tarot was the vice I was most eager to acquire and I soon found myself in a Borders bookstore, contemplating the locked glass case that sequestered the Tarot deck's concentrated occult essence from unsuspecting shoppers. Following the advice of various disreputable websites - and with my heart in my throat - I bought myself a classic Rider-Waite-Smith deck along with a basic text on Tarot symbolism.

Almost immediately the deck began to perplex and fascinate me. Though I was not, alas, possessed or even visited by demons, the cards did give me uncanny insight into my own psychological state and were occasionally and unmistakably prophetic.

As an example, I early on decided to deal myself one card that would give me insight into the coming year of my life. As I was shuffling a card sprang from the deck, seemingly of its own accord, and so I accepted it.

It was the Tower, a trump that augurs sudden change and in fact that single year saw dramatic transformations in my spirituality, career, and family. But even more than the accurate prediction the card's specific imagery spoke directly to me: it depicts a watchtower being destroyed by divine lightning. A man and a woman, separated by the tower, are falling headlong into a black abyss. The application to my own religious upheavals and the end of my marriage was, at times, unbearably poignant but also, at times, a source of grim relief - though harsh, the disruption was, at root, divine.

It is easy to dismiss this story as a vague coincidence or perhaps as a case of self-fulfilling prophecy and if it makes you feel better I encourage you to do just that. But it was *my* experience and *I* couldn't deny it so easily, though I wasted much time trying to believe in *some* comfortable explanation for the Tarot deck's inexplicable behavior. But uncanny examples kept accruing - for instance, one night I dreamt of a Tarot spread and the next morning I immediately shuffled the deck and dealt the cards I had just dreamed! In fact, like dreams, whenever I work with Tarot for more than a few days startling synchronicities pile up like firewood.

And again, I encourage you to *not* believe me - go and have your own weird experiences. But speaking for myself, I have been forced to accept that the future and the present are somehow entwined, that the world is irreducibly strange, and that sometimes wisdom really can be found 'in the cards'.

And this, I think, is the real reason that Tarot is so disliked by scientists, fundamentalists, and others caught up in rigid belief systems. Just fooling around with these 78 bits of pasteboard will, soon enough, provide personally irrefutable evidence that there are more things in heaven and earth than are accounted for in our puny dogmas, and when *that* Tower begins to crumble... the results can be very disturbing.

Marian Apparitions

Some of the most fascinating and persistent occult phenomena to afflict our planet are the continuing apparitions of the Blessed Virgin Mary - or BVM to us aficionados - who first began to appear to the faithful (and otherwise) in 352 A.D. and whose appearances continue in modern times.

It is natural for non-Catholics to assume that the Church has a vested interest in certifying Marian apparitions, to impress believers and non-believers alike. In fact, the opposite seems to be the case, and the elaborate bureaucracy and methodology for evaluating miracles conforms rather admirably to scientific method. The great majority of Marian apparitions - well over 95% - are flatly rejected because they don't meet the 'miracle investigators' high standards of proof. The miracles that remain, the intransigent few, are grudgingly dubbed 'worthy of belief'.

One of the approved apparitions, and my personal favorite, is Our Lady of Guadeloupe, who appeared in 1531 to the peasant Juan Diego of Guadeloupe, Mexico. The Lady asked Juan to be her messenger to the local Bishop and, charmingly, provided not one but two miracles of manifestation to aid poor Juan in his task. One of these, a bouquet of flowers produced in winter, is long gone but the other survives to our day and continues to awe the credulous and puzzle skeptics. It is an image of the Lady herself, printed or painted on Juan's *tilma*, an apron-like garment made of agave fiber. Though the tilma's fabric is quite coarse, the image on it is photographically crisp, with no visible brush marks. No one has satisfactorily explained how such precise work could have been done in 1531.

But even more astonishing is the *tilma's* very survival. Ordinarily, agave fabric disintegrates in 20 years or so, but for *475 years* the Guadeloupe relic has survived exposure to candle smoke, incense, and handling by many thousands of believers. Even the colors of the image remain surprisingly bright and clear which is, simply put, impossible. The frail fabric even survived, unscathed, a 1921 bombing that shattered the surrounding building.

So the image is one of these confounding things, a persistent, incarnate mystery, like the Patterson-Gimlin Bigfoot film or the Voynich Manuscript; they don't seem to really belong to our world and yet, unquestionably, they are in it.

When formulating an opinion about odd objects like the Guadeloupe image, it seems to me that there are two ways to go wrong. One is to reflexively deny the miraculous aspects of the object; the other is to accept it at face value.

Reflexive skepticism is a mistake because it pointlessly shrinks our world. It takes the mystery out of something that is, in fact, mysterious and, over time, diminishes our ability to accept the miraculous aspects of day to day existence.

Simple acceptance goes wrong by pretending to more certainty than is actually possible; after all, the *defining feature* of the Guadeloupe image is its inexplicability - and if we can't explain the object, it is mere hubris to pretend we understand its maker.

We have to find a middle ground between these two responses - to acknowledge the miraculous intrusions into our world, while not blindly accepting the intruders story at face value.

Bees: Smart Like Us?

The honeybee hive mind is one of the most sophisticated thinking machines on the planet, and even compares favorably with the thinking machine between our ears.

Hives store 50 pounds of honey in a season. To do this, hive workers complete about 4 million foraging trips, flying a total of 12 million miles. They systematically find dozens or hundreds of food patches, exploit them, and move on.

This is sophisticated stuff, requiring coordination at a level of complexity approaching that of a human corporation. In fact, bee intelligence is even capable of solving a mathematical series; in one experiment, entomologists placed a bowl of sugar water outside a hive. Bees quickly found it. The next day, the bowl was moved twice as far away. Again, the bowl was found. This went on for several days, with the bowl being moved away from the hive in a geometric, not arithmetic progression. The experiment was supposed to study search efficiency, but after several days something unexpected occurred; when the experimenters went to place the bowl, the bees had *anticipated them* and were already on the spot!

This is astonishing. There are, frankly, plenty of humans who have trouble with geometric progressions. How is it even possible for a *hive* to make this sort of calculation?

It is known that bees can communicate by means of the 'waggle dance', an abstract language that is eons older than any human language. Essentially, bees return to the hive and do the hokey-pokey; their jigs and jogs convey the precise location of food that may be miles away. In other words, they give each other good directions which, again, is not so common among humans. The dance's vocabulary is known

- there is even a dictionary; what is *not* known is how bees began to use such a sophisticated language.

Barbara Shipman, a mathematician at the University of Rochester, discovered that the shapes created during the waggle dance are the same as the shapes created when the possible curves of a 6 dimensional flag manifold are projected onto a 2 dimensional surface. Don't worry if you don't understand that - there are not many humans who do. The point is, there is a surprising, but real, correlation between an obscure branch of higher mathematics and the abstract language used by bees. Shipman even sees this as evidence that bees are able to sense quantum fields directly, a trick that human physicists believe to be impossible.

Be that as it may, bees certainly use abstract language to communicate, they are excellent navigators and planners, they can solve mathematical problems, and they manage food resources. What criteria for higher intelligence does this not meet?

Sadly, due to pesticide misuse, habitat reduction and mite infestations, honeybees are declining in the United States and could disappear entirely. The consequences are unknown - one possibility is agricultural collapse.

It may be, in fact, that the fate of the honeybee is bound up with the fate of our civilization, and that failure to appreciate their alien intelligence might lead to our own demise.

Another weird thing about DMT, and something that I couldn't squeeze into a three minute radio show, is the fact that it's amazingly common. It's found in dozens of plant species, notably in Reed Canary Grass which is one of the most widely distributed grasses on the planet - the odds are very good that you're sitting within a half mile of some right now. And, as these things go, it's fairly easy to synthesize or at least that's what I read on the Internet....

Oh, and another weird thing; that ripping sound that users often hear? A lot of UFO reports mention what appears to be the same sound, as do reports of Marian apparitions.

DMT

In 1990, Rick Strassman injected 60 people with 400 doses of the illegal drug dimethyltryptamine. But Strassman wasn't breaking any law - he was the first federally approved researcher in 20 years to study the effect of a psychedelic on human subjects.

Dimethyltryptamine - known as 'DMT' - is surely one of the strangest chemical substances found on our chemically rich planet. It is one of the strongest hallucinogens and even among veteran psychonauts it is spoken of with awe - gonzo drug theorist Terence McKenna used to say that the biggest danger of DMT is that a person could simply 'die of astonishment'. For one thing, DMT is one of the relatively few drugs that can produce true hallucinations, defined as virtual experiences that are indistinguishable from reality. And DMT is nearly unique in that it consistently delivers one of the strangest experiences humans have - encounters with aliens. In Strassman's study, 20% of those injected reported clear, detailed encounters with alien beings, all taking place in what the volunteers usually referred to as, 'another dimension'. That is, after injection with DMT, 1 in 5 of Strassman's subjects experienced entry into another plane of existence where they met aliens. Less formal 'trip reports' suggest that the ratio is much higher for those experimenting at home, and that the experience is even stronger when the drug is smoked rather than injected.

What's astonishing about the alien encounters is that they are incredibly weird and yet remarkably consistent. Nearly all users report a strange ripping sound and intricate radially symmetric visual phenomena as they enter 'DMT space'. They then report meeting astounding machine-like elves that are able to transform themselves at will, and are also able to modify reality by means of a weird language - in his lectures, McKenna even used to replicate this language.

So what is going on here? Other psychedelics, like LSD or psilocybin, create different trips in different people. But this drug seems to fairly often create the *same* trip in different people, even in people who are very different from each other. The ayahuasca shamans of South America, for example, have used DMT for thousands of years... and often encounter aliens.

 Could it be that these encounters are simply a mental fantasy created by this particular drug? Of course - humans know very little about the way hallucinogens work, largely because governments repress psychedelic studies.

But, could it be that DMT somehow precipitates a genuine trip to another dimension inhabited by self-transforming machine elves? Also of course - we know even less about aliens and other dimensions than we do about hallucinogens and brains.

And here is one more weird thing about DMT - you're on it right now. Dimethyltryptamine is found in small quantities in all human brains, possibly produced by the pineal gland. Scientists speculate that DMT plays a role in dreams and near death experiences, and possibly in the mystical religious visions that periodically alter humanity's course - the trip reports found in the Old Testament, for example, don't sound all that different from some DMT visions.

All human problems are rooted in human consciousness, and DMT consistently delivers the most radical possible expression of human consciousness... maybe we should keep looking into it.

E-Prime

"To be or not to be", Hamlet famously asked. Many scientists have come down strongly against 'be', not because they feel suicidal but because they subscribe to a theory of language known as "General Semantics". General Semantics posits that language and the rules that govern language profoundly affect our worldview, our thinking ability, and our very sense of self. It has steadily gained influence among scientists who find that it clarifies their thinking.

The theory teaches that some aspects of Standard English inevitably cause confusion in thinking. The verb 'to be' and the forms of 'to be' such as 'is' cause the most problems. When we say that one thing 'is' another thing we inevitably commit logical errors or pretend to more knowledge of a subject than we can actually have. For instance, consider the simple phrase, "You're an idiot". Taken literally, it can only mean that you somehow embody idiocy so profoundly that in every possible way and on every possible occasion you actually behave like an idiot, and it implies that every possible observer will agree that you always behave like an idiot. That seems unlikely, doesn't it, even for you?

To avoid the pesky 'be' verb, some people have learned to write and even speak and think in a subset of English known as E-Prime, defined as English minus all forms of 'be': is, are, were, was, am, be, been, and all their contractions. It seems paradoxical to improve a language by removing one of its major components, but in practice it works quite well.

In E-Prime, for example, if I want to call you an idiot, I have to go about it differently. I can't just say, "You're an idiot" because of the 'are' hiding in 'you're'. Instead I have to say something like, "You *seem* like an idiot to me" or maybe, "You just stepped in dog doodoo". Put like this, a more accurate picture emerges. Maybe *I* don't *understand* your genius. Maybe you just *like* dog doodoo.

Removing 'be' from our sentences forces us to describe events more exactly, more honestly. Writing things down in E-Prime forces us to clarify our thinking, reveals our unconscious assumptions, and often points to solutions that might never have occurred to us otherwise. E-Prime can change lives. For example, I used to spend the majority of my time in religious activity, but when I attempted to describe my beliefs in E-Prime, I found that I couldn't do so! *All* my beliefs rested on unconscious and unproven assumptions. Needless to say, this exercise gave me much food for thought. Try it yourself – just sit down and describe your personal philosophy without using any forms of the 'be' verb. I promise a truly enlightening experience.

For a primer on E-Prime go to nobeliefs.com/eprime, and for more about general semantics you can go to generalsemantics.org.

And if you think that E-Prime sounds like an interesting but unworkable idea, think again – I wrote *this* entire essay in E-Prime.

Ants & Mushrooms

nts and mushrooms are deeply fascinating. They are seemingly modest entities, small and almost literally beneath our notice. But they are not simple, nor are they unimportant. Ants, for example, are easily the most populous animal on the planet and their combined mass is many times that of humans. And fungi may be the most common living structure of all - there are an estimated 6 million varieties and some of them grow in large 'fungal mats' that cover as many as 20,000 acres with up to a *mile* of mycelial strands in a *single cubic inch* of soil.

And they communicate. Ants have a rich language based on pheromones and other chemical secretions that allow them to coordinate large activities - Army Ants, for example, engage in foraging raids and mass relocations in colonies numbering up to a million. There is even some evidence that ant colonies engage in propaganda wars and chemical disinformation. And fungal mycelia have been shown not only to respond to natural disasters such as fire, but to 'broadcast' the information so that other fungal networks can pick it up.

Scientists, frankly, know very little about all this complexity and tend to speak about it with awe. It's just so astounding to realize that these tiny little ants, these squishy little strands of fungus, are collectively so complex, so mind-numbingly beyond our current comprehension. When searching for metaphors, scientists come up with models of organization like cities, the Internet, or even the most complicated and organized object known, the human brain.

We're used to the idea that complexity adds up, that small beings can organize into big systems. Small unintelligent ants, for example, add up into large and sophisticated colonies, and individual humans add up into states and nations that can build telephone systems or send representatives to the moon. But systems add up as well; individuals add up to families, families add up to cities, cities add up to states, and so on and so on. Complex systems made up of smaller systems and beings seems to be a condition of life.

So what does *everything* add up to? All the human institutions, all the natural systems, all the ant colonies, all the fungal networks, all of the staggering complexity that coats the surface of this rocky planet... what is all *part* of?

The Gaia hypothesis, which holds that Earth can be viewed as a single organism, was first proposed in the 1970s. Initially it was ridiculed by those who held that it wasn't scientific, but so called 'weak' versions of the idea are now widely accepted. In retrospect, it seems sort of obvious: in a world full of biology frantically organizing into larger and larger systems, doesn't it seem possible that the world *itself* is a huge system?

Which brings us back to ants and mushrooms; they cover the surface of the planet with a net of complex structure, they exchange trillions of sophisticated chemical signals, they interact with other biological entities... if the scientists who are studying the Gaia hypothesis are looking for some mechanism by which the planet can 'think', a global 'brain', it seems to me like ants and mushrooms are a good place to start.

Cognitive Dissonance

C ognitive Dissonance" is a psychological poison, a dioxin of the mind that everyone should know about... but there are many who prefer that you *not* learn about it.

'Cognitive', of course, has to do with thinking, and 'dissonance' is stress created by disharmony. So cognitive dissonance is stress created when our inner world does not seem to be aligned with the outer world. Cognitive dissonance, in various forms, is a fundamental tool of all persuaders ranging from cult leaders, to advertisers, to... presidents.

Here is a personal example of cognitive dissonance in action. In the mid 1980s I was successfully recruited by a Christian fundamentalist cult. I attended a meeting and was greeted warmly – 'love-bombed'. Succumbing to peer pressure I joined in the prayers and songs, which naturally were based on the beliefs of this particular cult.

This created cognitive dissonance. The prayers and songs expressed beliefs that were quite a bit different from *my* beliefs, and yet... there I was, saying and doing things that I didn't believe. This inconsistency between actions and belief created dissonance. Though I wasn't consciously aware of it, the dissonance created stress that had to be resolved. This appears to be a fundamental law of human behavior.

Logically, there were two ways to resolve the stress. I could change what I was doing by walking out of the meeting, or... I could change my beliefs.

As it turned out, I chose to change my beliefs and, because of my new beliefs, I went to more meetings, which led to more adjustments to my belief, which led to... 17 years of my life wasted in a vicious feedback loop.

I'm lucky, or at least *relatively* lucky. Similar misuse of cognitive dissonance has led to atrocities such as the mass suicide of the Heaven's Gate cult.

Cognitive dissonance also works on a much broader scale. When a charismatic national leader, for example, insists continuously, loudly, and vigorously that the nation is threatened, history shows that many citizens will resolve the dissonance between what they experience and what they hear by adjusting their *experience* until they too feel threatened. This tactic worked for Hitler, and it's worked for American leaders as well.

Defense against cognitive dissonance is difficult. Intelligence is not enough. I qualify for MENSA, in case you care, but I still sold a lot of magazines door-to-door before I managed to remove my head from my rear. This is not unusual. Smart people seem to be especially good at coming up with clever defenses of bizarre beliefs.

But *awareness* can help. Just knowing the phrase 'cognitive dissonance' is a start. And being aware of common tactics is also a help. Here are a few: religious songs, patriotic songs, advertising ditties, pledges, oaths, public prayers, invocations, billboards, parades, infomercials, t-shirts, etc., etc., etc. If I make it sound like cognitive dissonance is potentially everywhere... well, it is. So be alert.

And there is at least one source of cognitive dissonance that you should be especially wary of, a danger that some claim is more insidious than any other. Yes, you should always be especially wary of... personal essays like this one.

Religious organizations, founded by and made up of humans, live far longer than any particular human. Buddhism and Roman Catholicism, for example, both claim to be about 2,000 years old... so today's believers are many, many generations removed from the impulses of those who got things started.

Is this a problem? Is it possible that the handing down of belief from one generation to the next leads to confusion, like a massive, centuries long game of telephone? Is it possible that as a religion gets older, it gets farther away from its roots? Does the survival of the organization become more important than the spiritual needs of its followers?

Should every generation make up their own religion?

I was thinking about these questions and a little story, a parable, occurred to me and I wrote it down as fast as I could. Frankly, it didn't feel like something I'd written, it felt like a gift... and here it is.

The Spring & the Pipeline

nce upon a time there was a village in the hills, suffering from drought. The villagers searched for water and found, miraculously it seemed, a fresh pure spring high in the hills and far away. They were so happy. Though it was a difficult journey, they went to the spring often, to drink at the source and to haul back what they needed for day to day use.

But eventually they began to notice that it was a quite a long trip and that it was difficult to bring back all that they needed. So they conceived of a pipeline, the greatest task they could ever set for themselves, and with great effort and after many false starts they were able to build it and it made them happy. Now they could have water from the spring right in their village.

Now the villagers were the first to admit that their pipeline was not perfect. Having no other material at hand, they were forced to use thin bamboo that limited the flow and the tar they used to seal the joints could give the water a funny taste now and then. So, although they were happy with their pipeline, some of the villagers would journey up to the spring on occasion, to drink pure water from the source.

Time passed, and eventually all those who had discovered the spring and built the pipeline passed on. Their children had been told about the spring, and they believed in it. After all, they could see the proof of its existence in the steady supply of water that was delivered to their village. Few of them had actually been to the source, but they appreciated the funny tasting water and the pipeline, and they were content.

Still more time passed and the flow of water began to wane and it even stopped at times. The villagers assumed that the spring was dying away – but they could never have thought this if they had seen the beautiful spring for themselves. In reality, the pipeline was failing because it was old and because it was being neglected.

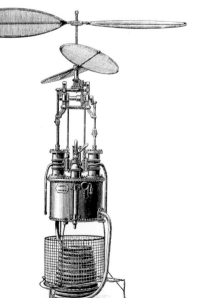

The villagers began to grumble and to doubt everything they had ever been told. Needing water, some moved to other villages. Most of those who remained tried to live off of the water that still came through the pipeline, though it was scarce now, and foul tasting. A few, a very few, went searching and exploring, and followed the old pipeline far back into the hills and discovered the spring for themselves, as full and as fresh and as pure as it had ever been.

And they were very happy.

We Are A.I.

iction precedes fact in our mediated society. Cyrano de Bergerac, for example, wrote of travel to the moon long before humans actually accomplished it. Fiction is now taking us to stranger places than the moon - my favorite example, the Matrix Trilogy, forced millions of viewers to seriously consider the possibility that our world is in fact virtual, a vast computer construct, and that all of us living here are complex programs.

In science, *controversy* precedes fact. New ideas are usually attacked by the reigning establishment, and are only accepted if they prove, over time, to explain more than prevailing ideas. Thus, Darwin's theory of evolution replaced the theory of acquired traits because it explained fossil evidence that was otherwise mysterious.

Some scientists and philosophers are now proposing a crazy theory that I rather like; they suggest that we *really do* live in a Matrix type world, because the *odds* favor it. Their reasoning goes something like this:

Artificial intelligence is likely to happen. Humans have only been messing around with computers for a few decades, and have already come rather close to achieving genuine machine entities. So it can be assumed that in a few decades humans will create actual artificial intelligences, computer beings with free will and self-consciousness. But they will still be, in essence, programs. And programs can be copied and distributed infinitely. So shortly after one A.I. exists, *millions* will exist, all living independent lives and presumably interacting with each other. And all those A.I.s will have some conception of the world, will perceive themselves to be in some sort of complex universe with time and space - after all, to *be* you need space to be, and time to be, even if space and time are illusions.

Consider this alongside another fact: our Sun is one of trillions of stars, and it's relatively young. Not only do the odds favor the existence of other intelligent beings, the odds also suggest that they are older than us - *millions of years* older than us. So their experimentation with computers took place a long time ago, and the artificial intelligences they created have been replicating all that time.

This chain of reasoning leads to the conclusion that A.I.s vastly outnumber 'natural' beings... which leads to the conclusion that *we* are A.I.s, living in a virtual world, since that is the most likely possibility.

This idea is appearing over and over in art; in the Matrix and other movies, in books, and most of all in video games where we actually experience vivid digital worlds with different rules than our own.

And viewing the world we live in as virtual also explains a lot of anomalies that puzzle science. For example, scientists have no good theories to explain why mathematical formulas describe reality so well... but if the world is a vast computer program this phenomenon is *easily* explained.

A virtual world also accounts for spiritual riddles that science won't touch. Mystics tell us that time and space are illusions and that there is an inescapable underlying unity - and of course these statements are true if the world is all bits on a hard drive.

So it may be true that we all live on some equivalent of a computer hard drive, but it may also be true that it doesn't matter - after all, virtual or not, this *is* our reality.

Patty Hearst

atricia Campbell Hearst, better known as Patty Hearst, was kidnapped by members of the so called Symbionese Liberation Army on February 4, 1974. She was 19. Two months later she was photographed holding an assault rifle during a San Francisco bank robbery. It was learned that she had changed her name to Tania, denounced her parents, and proudly claimed to be a full-fledged member of the SLA. Patty/Tania was captured in September of 1975 and on February 4th, 1976, exactly 2 years after her kidnapping, she was brought to trial. Here's where her story gets *really* interesting.

Patty Hearst and her lawyer, F. Lee Bailey, claimed that she was not guilty because she had been subjected to extreme brainwashing techniques including isolation, brutality, milieu control and psychological manipulation. Prosecutors didn't deny that these things happened, they merely contended that Patty had been a willing victim and became a believing member of the SLA. Jurors apparently agreed and found her guilty. She was sentenced to 25 years.

American opinion was divided at the time, and is divided today. *Can* a person be brainwashed into committing violent crime? Having committed the crime, is such a person guilty?

The techniques of brainwashing - or 'coercive persuasion' - have been well known for centuries, and are even the subject of scholarly study. Patty Hearst's ordeal was not terribly different from the experience of many Americans who have survived the ordeal known as 'boot camp' and of course the goal of both ordeals is exactly the same - conversion to a new belief system, a belief system that makes it possible to kill or face death in the service of a particular ideology. In milder form, some techniques of coercive persuasion are used by religions, businesses, political parties and even families - a case could be made that *all* humans have been at least mildly brainwashed, merely by being born into a particular family and culture... after all, what parent doesn't attempt to raise their child with the *parent's* values? The fact is, brainwashing in one form or another is fairly common and rather effective.

President Carter commuted Patty's sentence and 5 years after her kidnapping she was released. On January 20th, 2001, on the last day of his presidency, Bill Clinton granted her a full pardon for all crimes. Patty Hearst, officially an innocent woman, now lives quietly in Connecticut.

This case holds a peculiar fascination for me because of the 17 years I spent in a fundamentalist Christian cult. From personal experience I can attest that even mild forms of coercive persuasion can be effective - at least on me. I didn't commit any crimes as a cult member, but I certainly did things to be ashamed of, and I don't find it easy to pardon myself. It *was* me that did those things. And Patty Hearst *did* carry a gun during armed robberies, and on at least one occasion she shot that gun.

So is she guilty? Or, are her kidnappers the guilty ones? What if her kidnappers had been subjected to some form of brainwashing? Would the blame for Patty's crimes have to keep leapfrogging back in time, in search of a criminal untainted by brainwashing? What if no such criminal exists?

What if guilt... is just a word?

After I'd been writing the radio show for a while, I had an itch to sum it up, to state in a few words what Belief Systems and Other B.S. *was really <u>about</u>. The following essay is the result, so much so that Skip Naft, the show's producer, took to calling this particular essay the 'crux of the biscuit' - whatever that means.*

Belief Systems

hen I was about 15, I got serious about bird-watching and studied birds obsessively. Because I lived in a Los Angeles suburb, I assumed that the local birding wouldn't be very good and I would travel for hours to more exotic spots. But after a few weeks I began to notice all sorts of birds right in my yard - lots of woodpeckers, vireos, thrashers, several species of hawk...

The birds, of course, had been there all along. But I couldn't *see* them until I became aware of the possibility of their existence, until I learned the language associated with their appearance. By expanding my inner world, I expanded and enriched my outer world.

Our sets of assumptions about the world - our belief systems - dramatically affect our experience of the world. Consider a less trivial example; several studies have shown that patient expectations about a drug or therapy strongly affect the performance of the drug or therapy. That is, if you *expect* a pill to work, the odds are better that it will. But if you don't think the pill is going to work, it may not.

This being the case, we'd all be better off *believing* that we're going to be cured - in other words, learning to manage our belief systems is a valuable skill that will enhance and even extend our lives. In other other words, beliefs are a *choice* - they aren't built into us, they aren't forced upon us, they're something we *choose...* and some of us choose exceptionally lousy beliefs.

The aftermath of Hurricane Katrina offers another lesson about belief systems. Several religious organizations declared that Katrina was divine retribution from their versions of the deity. Environmentalists declared that Katrina was evidence for global warming. Democrats saw massive evidence of government ineptitude, and Republicans saw massive evidence that more money should be given to Halliburton and that the Iraq war should definitely continue. Every group with access to a microphone had their own interpretation of what Katrina meant; that it might have no meaning at all was never publicly considered.

So one man's divine retribution is another man's natural disaster and yet another man's political point and the only difference between all these men is their belief systems.

The title of this show (and book), "Belief Systems & Other B.S.", is taken from the writings of cult philosopher Robert Anton Wilson who has spent much of his life adopting and analyzing various belief systems - that is, he doesn't just *study* belief systems he, um, *believes* them and then gauges the effect of the Belief System on his own happiness. This has led him down some mighty strange roads and Wilson says it's no coincidence that the phrase 'Belief Systems' can be shortened to 'B.S.'

And what are Wilson's conclusions after a lifetime of extreme philosophy? He has distilled them down to a couple of principles, also known as Wilson's Laws:

1) Never believe totally in other people's B.S.

2) Never believe totally in your *own* B.S.

And I should add a third law for readers - never believe totally in *Belief Systems and Other B.S.*

It's All About You... or Maybe Me

Solipsism is the philosophical idea that there is only one consciousness, one being, and everything that exists is somehow created by this one consciousness who may or may not be aware that he (or she) is the only *truly* conscious being. In other words, all the other supposed beings are in fact just projections of this one person's mind. Solipsism is famously hard to disprove because we can never be positive that the people around us really exist - they may just be the external equivalent of voices in our heads. Think about the people in your dreams. They talk to you, don't they? They seem to have personalities, and they do things that surprise you, don't they? And what about the world around you in dreams? Your dream world may be weird, true, but it *is* a world. That is, the people and things you experience in dreams are detailed and

convincing and seem to have their own logic - just like they do in the world you call the *real* world. So how can you be sure that the so-called real world isn't just another version of your dream world - a convincing but self-created fantasy?

But if it's hard to *disprove* solipsism, it's also pretty hard to *prove* - after all, who does one prove it *to*? Since I know that *I* am conscious and self-aware, trying to convince *you* that solipsism is true is kind of pointless, isn't it? Why should I waste my time trying to convince you that you're just a projection of my mind and have no independent reality?

But, what if *you* are the only conscious being, and I'm a projection of *your* consciousness, a figment of your imagination? I could be, you know. This essay could be a subtle ploy of your own design, a way to remind yourself that *you* are the only truly conscious being and the rest of us are as insubstantial as characters in a dream. Of course, if you were to start thinking that, *I'd* know you were crazy, because *I* know that I'm real... but how would *you* know that you're crazy?

But the important question about solipsism is not, 'is it true?' but, 'does it matter?' That is, suppose you *are* the only truly conscious being, living in a world that you've forgotten creating. What possible difference could it make to the way you live your life? You still have to deal with the rest of us, just like you have to deal with persistent thoughts over which you seem to have no control - you know, like when you can't get that Ricky Nelson song, *Garden Party* out of your head?

And there's another interesting question; what if solipsism is a *good* thing? If you consistently view the world as your own creation, you at least are taking responsibility for it. Granted, you may not have done a very good job of creation so far but, starting now, you can change all that. True, it is but a brief step from responsible solipsism to full-blown psychosis... but, nothing ventured, nothing gained.

So, solipsists of the world unite! You have nothing to lose but your self-inflicted chains!

No Bulk

hysicists tell us that there is no bulk, there is only information. 'Matter' is made of molecules, and molecules are made of atoms, and atoms are made of subatomic particles and subatomic particles aren't particles at all, they're waveforms, or probabilities, or concepts, or *something* but they're definitely *not* little marbles that bounce off of each other. We can say they're energy, whatever that means, but we can also say they're information, bits of code that interact with other bits of code in predictable ways that cumulatively add up to what we optimistically call the 'laws' of nature.

This is non-intuitive. Deep down, most of us live in a Newtonian world where gravity controls everything and the apple in our hand is made of tiny tinkertoy molecules. If we think at all about atoms, we tend to visualize them as miniature solar systems, with electrons and positrons orbiting a nucleus. This is the picture often presented in school textbooks, but it is astoundingly wrong - there *is* no way to effectively visualize subatomic structures because they don't *look* like anything.

Acknowledging this truth, letting it sink in, can be a little frightening because it means that we live in a world with, literally, no solid ground; everything we observe is made up of intangible mystery and we ourselves, the observers, are made up of intangible mystery.

The fact is, we live in a completely inscrutable world, a world where literally anything can be true. For if there are no little bits of matter, most of the limits we place on reality are meaningless. A world without bulk is a world where realities can overlap and William Blake was merely being observant when he said,

> *"... a World in a Grain of Sand*
> *And a Heaven in a Wild Flower*
> *Hold Infinity in the palm of your hand*
> *And Eternity in an hour."*

In fact, Blake and all the other visionary mystics that have graced humanity's existence seem to be on to something - their visions of deep unity, of paradises and other realms existing along side our quotidian lives, of immortal selves that transcend the body, are more in line with the true nature of reality than the Newtonian sleep of our daily existence.

Many of the phenomena that so puzzle us are easily explained by a world in which anything is possible. The UFOs that are seen by 1,000s every year, the supernatural intrusions of gods, demons and ghosts, the mysteries of crop circles, Bigfoot, dark matter and, well, *everything* can all be as firmly grounded in the same sort of fungible reality that *we* exist in.

But suppose all this folderol is actually the case, and we really *do* live in a world of overlapping realities and mystic visions... what's in it for us? If any conceivable reality is as potentially real as the one we live in, what prevents us from living in a reality that conforms in every way to our personal vision of a perfect world? As near as I can tell, the answer is... nothing prevents us, nothing at all.

Sarcasm

I am sarcastic. My sense of humor is ironic, and I often make deadpan comments that are quite amazingly funny. However, not everyone finds me amusing and, frankly, this has always puzzled me. It is usually obvious, to me at least, that I am being astoundingly hilarious, and yet sometimes the people I'm talking to aren't laughing. It's a mystery.

Recent medical studies shed some light on this conundrum. A team of Israeli researchers studied 41 victims of brain injury, along with 17 people who were 'normal' - that is, not brain damaged. Sarcastic and non-sarcastic versions of a story were read to participants and then they were asked about the meaning of the stories. In other words, researchers wanted to know if the participants were 'getting it' - a position I have often been in myself.

It turned out that subjects with a certain *type* of brain damage - to the prefrontal lobe - were pretty much incapable of understanding sarcasm. The researchers suggest that understanding sarcasm depends on a complex sequence of events in which the brain's language areas determine the literal meaning of the words and the frontal lobes and right hemisphere process emotional content, with the prefrontal lobe integrating the meaning. So sarcasm, as *I* have often said, is sophisticated business.

The article didn't say what the researchers did with the participants who didn't understand sarcasm - I suppose they were taken out and shot to put them out of their misery. But the study raises disturbing questions about personality, and even about the soul. A couple of years ago, for example, I had a small stroke that damaged my optic nerve, leaving me partially blind. That was certainly inconvenient, but it didn't make me feel that I had become a different person; it just made me feel like a somewhat reduced version of my essential self.

But what if the damage had been in my prefrontal area, in the all-important 'sarcasm center'? What if my ability to create and understand sarcasm had been affected? This *would* affect my essential self - my soul, if you like; honestly, without sarcasm, much of reality would be simply unbearable for me and I would no longer be a source of the incredibly perceptive humor for which I am noted.

And even worse things can happen as a result of brain damage. There is a very well documented case, for example, of a mid-life stroke turning a previously admirable man into a determined pedophile. Some variety of brain damage had turned him into a monster. Who is to blame in a case like this? If personality and even morality are at the mercy of brain damage, is it fair to blame *anyone* for an evil act? Maybe they're just victims of brain damage. Maybe they should be pitied.

But the important thing is that the article helped me to understand why some people don't get my humor. This very essay, for example, contains some really choice nuggets of sarcasm that maybe you didn't find amusing. In the past this would really bother me and I would wonder if maybe I could have written it better or been funnier. But now I don't have to worry about any of that. Now, if you don't get my humor, I'll know that it's not *me*, it's *you*. You're brain damaged.

Wizards of Ozs

man is walking on a lonely country road. A mysterious craft appears, carrying strange little people. Then he blacks out, recovering days later with only hazy memories of what actually happened to him. As time goes by, he gradually remembers some details and becomes a changed man, a mystic, spouting prophetically in a manner that strikes his former friends as deranged.

It sounds like a UFO abduction case, doesn't it, but in fact the same description could apply to stories of Faerie which once were all the rage in the British Isles. Faerie lore is as rich and strange as the modern UFO phenomenon, persisted for hundreds of years and, like UFOlogy, is blessed - or cursed - with a curious mixture of highly credible eyewitness accounts, puzzling physical evidence, inconclusive prophesy, and at least a few outright hoaxes.

But even Faerie tales have historical precedents: anyone who has read, say, the Greek Myths or the ancient Hebrew Scriptures will be familiar with tales of angels, demons and gods who appear as strange beings in strange craft, and whose appearances to humans are often accompanied by visions, lost time and, if we are honest about it, a healthy dash of outright terror. And here again we find the perplexing mix of dubious evidence, inexplicable events, and bamboozlement that characterize UFO sightings today.

Extraterrestrials were never a particularly good explanation for the UFOs that have infested our skies since about the 1950s; there was always, for example, the problem of motivation, along with the clumsy brutality of abductions, the multiplicity of alien species and craft, and of course the big question - if aliens *really* want to get to know us, why don't they just land on the White House lawn and get it over with? As prominent UFO analyst Jacques Vallee has said, "I will be disappointed if UFOs turn out to be nothing more than spaceships." And this view is increasingly common among long-time UFO researchers - more and more, the phenomenon seems to be taking on occult and religious trappings that have little to do with interplanetary travel.

Which leads us to a Grand Unified Theory of occult phenomena: suppose that *all* visitations - all the angels and demons, the faeries, the gods and even all the alien types - the grays,

the dwarfs, the Nordics and so forth and, oh heck, lets throw in Bigfoot and Nessie as well - suppose they are just the material manifestation of some deeper phenomena, some class of marginally physical intelligence that, for its own inscrutable reasons, chooses to interact with humans in a way that alternately terrifies and exalts us, leads us on and then dashes all hope of certainty. My postulated intelligences would thus be something like the Wizard of Oz - always behind the scenes, always manipulating appearances but, ultimately, comprehensible and even mundane.

I admit my theory is rather limited - it's not an explanation that actually *explains* much - but it is at least a place to start. Rather than being endlessly distracted by the current variants of our manipulators, perhaps we can start to examine the underlying similarities... and maybe, someday, we might get to the bottom of it all.

Dark Matter

Have you ever lost your wallet? Embarrassing, isn't it? Scientists have a similar problem; it seems they can't find most of the, um, universe. More than 90% of everything seems to be... missing.

The problem came to light in 1933 when astronomer Fred Zwicky measured the mass of galaxies by using their brightness to estimate the number of stars, and thus the galaxy's mass. Then he used a different method to estimate mass based on the velocity of stars in the outer rim of galaxies – the answer he got was *400 times greater* than the answer based on the brightness method.

The problem is, galaxies spin rapidly, but don't fall apart. They are like our solar system, but on a much larger scale. If our solar system didn't have the Sun at the center, the planets wouldn't orbit; they'd just fly off into space like a child being thrown from a merry-go-round. Similarly, galaxies are made up of stars held together by *something*, but that *something* doesn't seem to exist. Put simply, there's a whole bunch of stuff out there that humans can't find.

That stuff is called dark matter, and there are two main theories as to what it might be. It could be massive dark objects - like brown dwarf stars or black holes - that have mass but are hard to see. The problem is, current technology such as the Hubble space telescope, *can* detect brown dwarfs and black holes... and there aren't nearly enough of them.

The other theory is that there are a lot of WIMPs in the universe. WIMP stands for Weakly Interacting Massive Particles. The theory is that these are subatomic particles that don't interact with what we call normal matter. Physicists now think that WIMPs are the best candidate for resolving the dark matter problem.

But there's some delicious irony here; if WIMPs are real, their total mass is a *lot* more than the mass of what we call normal matter... in fact, *WIMPs are normal*, and everything that humans can see and interact with is sort of... unusual.

Just a few hundred years ago humans had to accept the fact that the world didn't revolve around us, it revolved around the Sun. Later, we had to accept that the Sun isn't a particularly big star and even our galaxy is small potatoes compared to the rest of the universe. Now we have to deal with the idea that the entire universe as we know it is small potatoes compared to... well we don't *know* what to compare it to. By definition, it's hard to even *interact* with WIMPs, let alone know much about them.

So science tells us of a vast, unknowable world, present but unseen, just out of range of our most sophisticated instruments. Hmmmm... it sounds a little religious doesn't it? After all if there's nothing, really, that we *can* say about the non-normal world of dark matter, it's also true that there's nothing we *can't* say. Speculation about heaven, the Tao, astral planes, other dimensions, disembodied intelligence... could all be true.

Science and religion both try to figure out the place of humans in the world, and it's interesting that they both seem to be ending up in the same place... completely flummoxed by mysterious worlds we can't even see.

Now, if you'll excuse me, I have to go find my wallet.

Corporate Beings

The time has come to think of corporations as living entities, as beings with desires and abilities quite apart from the desires and abilities of the human beings of which they are comprised. I believe that corporations are beings made up of humans in the same way that humans are beings made up of cells. Corporations, after all, live longer than us, pursue goals that seem crazy to us, and in many ways seem to resent and work against us. They are certainly harder to *kill* than humans.

It's not my belief, though, that corporations are *necessarily* 'bad', though certainly that's the way to bet. I only argue that they should be recognized as powerful beings in their own right. Whether or not this is true in any objective sense, it is true in the sense that it is a useful viewpoint, the one that helps us to best understand corporations.

If we do begin to consider corporations as beings, we can then begin to observe them as biologists observe anthills, or as anthropologists study alien cultures - that is, scientifically, with the goal of increasing our understanding of these remarkable entities that exist among us. Increasing our understanding might eventually help us to control them so that they more often work on our behalf.

One observation I have made is that corporations are fanatical about spreading their brand, their corporate iconography. Consider all the infinite crap that corporations plaster with logos: stationery, football games, cards, posters, shoes, T-shirts, billboards, cars, TV shows, buses, planes, blimps, Tiger Woods, mugs, computers and on and on and *on* and on. Or consider stadium naming rights; Minute Maid recently agreed to pay the Houston Astros *$170 million* for the rights to have their logo attached to a new stadium. The ostensible reason, of course, is that advertising brings in customers, but what if that's just a side effect of the *real* motivation - to mark out territory with corporate symbolism just as dogs mark out territory with urine? I know it sounds crazy and I don't know how it can be proved but it makes intuitive sense to me and I believe it's a hypothesis worth exploring.

This peculiar belief of mine also applies, of course, to religions and governments. They're like three mutations of the same beast, or three heads of the same monster, all long lived entities made up of humans, all pursuing inhuman agendas, and they all spread their symbolism obsessively. Icon, flag, logo... in essence, aren't they all exactly the same? All outposts in the battle for market share in the human mind space?

If I am right, then one way to limit the growth and influence of these often malignant entities is to fight the spread of their iconography into public space, to fight it as vigorously as we fight any graffiti. No logos, no crosses or crescents, no flags, just public space blessedly free of manipulative symbolism. Of course, if I am right, these more-than-human entities will fight back, and perhaps it will be the beginning of the final conflict between us and them.

I say, bring it on. Smaller governments, weaker corporations, and a lot less religion will surely bring about happier humans and a more peaceful world.

Criticism

I went to see Richard III with my daughter... you know, by Shakespeare? I hoped, of course, that the Bard's exalted words would bless and inform us both but as it turned out the acting, staging, and directing were all equally bad, so instead we discovered the joy of leaving a play early together.

It was fun. We were there for nearly half an hour until it dawned on me that *I* was sticking it our for *her* sake and that she was doing the same, so I finally leaned over to suggest that enough was enough and she, rather quickly, agreed. So we left, stepping on toes as we clambered out of our mid-row seats, accidentally slamming the theatre doors, and then si-

dling past snooty attendants until we were finally *free*, giggling and saying repeatedly to each other, "That Shakespeare guy, he sucks!"

I was a little worried that Janét would feel bad about leaving early and perhaps offending the actors who are, after all, people with feelings. But she viewed our exit as valuable feedback for the performers. 'How else would they know they suck?' she asked reasonably.

How else indeed? If everyone who performed was praised merely for their effort, with nothing but friendly words for even a poor performance, then excellence would be extremely rare. Critics serve humanity. They are like the wolves who keep the caribou herds strong by eating the slow and the sick – eating poor performers is surely an ultimate form of criticism.

So critics are a condition of excellence, not merely carping parasites. Muckraking journalists are critics. Wolves and other predators are critics. People leaving plays early are critics. And they all do a great service. Too often, I think, we look for something nice to say, teach our children to be 'positive', when skillful criticism would probably do more to increase the sum of human happiness. Unthinking niceness fosters only mediocrity.

There are other good reasons to learn the art of leaving early, along with the allied arts of giving up on a bad book or ending a dull conversation. In the course of a lifetime, these simple skills save months of boredom. Leaving early also requires boldness. The child who can clamber out of a crowded row during a performance has learned that sometimes it is a good thing to 'step on toes'.

And there is something else… leaving early demands respect for one's own happiness, which is the same as self-respect. Leaving a lousy play early can be rehearsal for leaving a lousy job or poisonous relationship.

My daughter and I enjoyed our escape. We got some burgers, we dissed Shakespeare, we had a serious conversation about what could have been improved… it was quality time.

So, teach your children to give up, to quit, to escape – you'll be doing them and the rest of us a great service.

Crop Circles

I happen to be a Registered Land Surveyor, licensed in the State of Wisconsin. I am, therefore a government certified expert in the art of laying out large patterns, such as subdivisions, on the ground. Which brings me, naturally, to crop circles.

My musings on crop circles usually take the form of an imaginary client who walks into my office and asks me if I could lay out a large pattern in a wheat field. "Sure", I say, "I have the equipment and personnel to do that." But then he says, "Well, the work has to be done all in one night. And you have to mash the wheat down neatly, without breaking it off - in fact, you have to bend it a few inches above the ground and weave it into a basket pattern. There will be people looking for you but you can't be seen and you can't leave footprints. The pattern I want you to make is quite large, several hundred feet across, and it's kind of complicated. Oh and, by the way, it's not my field - and the farmer has threatened to shoot trespassers."

So I show my imaginary client to the imaginary door in my mind, but then I get to thinking... jeez, *could* I lay out a crop circle, given the above conditions? And you know what? Maybe. Maybe I could if I had a big crew and practiced a lot, and if the field was lit and it was dry... but then I think, no way. Not if the farmer wasn't cooperating. Not without being seen.

But the fact is, at least *some* formations are hoaxed, and by some very talented people. Working for pay, some hoaxers have made very large formations as advertisements or for TV programs. But... all the formations that have *definitely* been hoaxed were made in the daytime, on rented fields, with the help of large booms so that the formation could be seen from above.

Here are a few things that *haven't* happened: no hoaxer has ever announced a complex pattern in advance, no hoaxer has ever been caught in the act, no hoaxer has ever been interrupted and left a large pattern half-finished, and no hoaxer has ever demonstrated on camera a good technique for creating the often extraordinary weavings formed by the bent crop.

In the end, beliefs about crop circles are a lot like beliefs about Bigfoot, the Illuminati, aliens, and God. One has to consider the swirl of evidence and counter-evidence, and make a decision. As always, only fools and madmen are ever absolutely certain.

Well, you've read this far; it seems only fair to tell you where *I* stand on the issue of crop circles. I believe that conventional hoaxers don't account for all crop circles. I believe that at least some crop circles cannot be explained by use of any known human technology. I believe that crop circles are a manifestation of some advanced intelligence. And, most of all, I believe that a crop circle tattoo on the left ankle is a good way to secure a position of oversight in the post alien takeover world.

Loyalty Cards

Grocery store 'loyalty cards', besides having a creepy name, are a form of corporate abuse against customers. Card systems cost millions to introduce and maintain and, because there ain't no such thing as a free lunch, that cost is added directly to food costs so that 'reduced' food costs end up being about the same as the suggested retail price. In other words, the card 'sale' price is roughly equivalent to the pre-card regular price, and the new regular prices are higher than they used to be. Your total grocery bill, after card system deployment, is higher by several percent – which is a funny way to reward loyalty.

Grocery store chains know full well that they aren't actually buying or rewarding 'loyalty' – after all, most consumers carry multiple loyalty cards. And, after all costs are counted, they have a hard time actually making money from the systems. So why do they all use them? There are at least two reasons. First, they do it because all the other chains are doing it – as soon as one chain drank the Kool-Aid, all the others had to have a glass as well. But second, there is a very concrete benefit to the chains – they are able to gather detailed information on the buying patterns of their customers, and use that information to extract more money from them. This is done by a sinister marketing technology known as customer segmentation. Segmentation allows stores of all kinds to identify their most profitable customers, find out what they like to buy, and offer them more of it. So if you're wealthy, or if you have a large family and no time, you're likely to see more of the foods that you like to buy at your store, more of which will be on sale. And you may get special savings, such as a discounted tank of gas. The upshot is, about one third of a store's customers will get lower prices, while the majority of us who aren't in large families, aren't wealthy, or aren't ro-botic con-sumer droids will pay high-er prices.

But wait, it gets better! The information collected is not legally protect-ed and can be made available on request to police agencies and other government bureaus. It can even be sold to other corporations who are interested in your buying habits. So you're not being paranoid, Big Brother is real... and he wants to sell you stuff.

So, if you're having trouble following along, here's how it stands. Grocery chains have installed so-called loyalty card systems that register us, spy on us, and financially screw most of us – and, in a stroke of evil genius, they make us pay for it all.

You should learn more about this racket by going to an excel-lent website, www.nocards.org.

Can you fight back? Of course you can. First of all, buy as di-rect and local as possible, and try to avoid the abusive system entirely. Second, raise heck. Tell the managers at your local store that you feel cheated and abused by the card system and ask for sale prices without having to use the card. Third, hayduke the system by trading cards with anyone willing. You *can* make a difference – some large chains have already dropped loyalty cards due to customer resistance.

And, for the record, I hereby declare myself willing to trade cards with anyone who asks.

Termites & Me

Termite mounds are famously complex - they have cooling and aeration systems, food factories, waste disposal arrangements and all the other *accoutre-mént* of a large city. The puzzle, of course, is how termites can build and maintain such sophisticated systems. They are, after all, bugs. Certainly there is no *individual* termite smart enough to design a termite mound; and can termites even *appreciate* the beauty and complexity of the world they've made for themselves?

I am part of a complex structure. I have a share in a small irrigation ditch. To keep our little ditch maintained requires a lot of high quality thinking - not by me - along with some manual labor that's as hard as, well, ditch digging. The complexity of this single ditch is just about the limit of my understanding. But our ditch is one of several that draw from one reservoir, and, of course, the reservoirs themselves are part of a complex system... and all of this has been in place for several decades and parts have been around for more than a hundred years. My relationship to the water system in my area is like the relationship of a termite to its mound: I depend on it, but I have no idea how it works... I'm just happy that there are people who can tell me where to dig. There probably isn't *any* one person that comprehends all of the myriad complexities of even my local water system. There are people who understand the legalities, people who understand the engineering, people who understand the watersheds, and people like me who pretty much understand shovels... but are there people who understand all of it? I don't think so.

But a water system is simple compared to the complexity of a large city, or a computer network, or a language. The fact is, modern humans depend on self-created systems that we can't entirely comprehend or even appreciate.

When we look at natural systems like a termite mound - or a coral reef, or an aspen grove, or *whatever* - we usually feel that we're looking *down* on something. That humans are at the top of some sort of hierarchy because of our intelligence. It's true that our intelligence has enabled us to assemble the most exquisitely complicated structures that we are able to observe, but it's also true that termites could say the same thing. After all, if termites were to build a mound in the middle of a city, they would not be able to 'observe' the complexity around them. It wouldn't be part of their world.

So why are we so sure that we're at the 'top' of anything? The fact is, hierarchies of complexity that surpass understanding seem to be more or less a condition of life. And most of the systems that we can observe are made up of simple beings that have little or no concept of our existence.

So I've been wondering lately, when I dig a ditch, or use a telephone, or visit a big city, if there might not be some super-intelligent observer looking at me and marveling, wondering how such a primitive being managed to create such a beautiful system.

In other words, I've been wondering if I'm that much different from a termite in a mound.

Cabala Conspiracies

The ancient and voluminous Hebrew mystic methodology known as 'Cabala' contains many wonders and can even be stretched to contain, just barely, the ignorant maunderings of Madonna and others of her celebrity ilk. But the aspect of Cabala that typically captures the interest of Western mathematicians, theologians and other librarians of the invisible is Gematria, the alphanumeric system used to investigate and catalog the nature of God as revealed in language and other data. Those who practice Gematria rejoice in the seemingly more than coincidental associations between aspects of reality that one expects to be completely *un*related. As an example, Gematria delights in the fact that there are exactly 22 solid figures that can be composed from regular polygons. This mathematical trivia is then considered along with the fact that there are exactly 22 letters in the Hebrew alphabet, and exactly 22 pathways on the Cabalistic Tree of Life and from there the Cabalist can spend days, months or years deciding which solids should be assigned to which pathway. At first blush, Gematria can seem obsessive but a little study reveals profound beauty in the lengthy chains of association and ultimately Gematria seems no more insane than the mystic theology of *any* religion and a fairly reliable technology for demonstrating to the adherent that, in fact, everything *is* connected to everything else and that our feelings of separateness are illusory.

Cabalists traditionally had a strained relationship with conventional Jewish religion and were generally viewed as odd intellectuals pursuing unlikely coincidences with little meaning in the 'real world', whatever *that* might be. In this respect they are very like today's conspiracy theorists, who also sift language obsessively, looking for the connections between worldly phenomena that appear, on the surface, to be completely unrelated. And, like cabalists, as we conspiracy theorists progress in our studies, we also find that, indeed, everything *is* connected to everything so that, for example, the annual hijinks at the Bohemian Grove can be traced back to Egyptian initiatory ritual and forward to Freemasonry and the JFK assassination and from there sideways to Aleister Crowley and Jack Parsons whose Amalantrah and Babalon workings invoked the entity Lam and ripped a void in the etheric planes that opened the way for the modern UFO phenomenon and the military industrial complex which - by constructing the High-frequency Active Aural Research Project, HAARP, - have brought about most of the modern weather disasters and earthquakes not to mention 9/11 which has numerological associations linking it to the star Sirius and the

Secret Chiefs and... well, let's not even get started on ritual child abuse, MK-ULTRA, Project Paperclip and chemtrails. In fact, lets not only not get started let's not even acknowledge that we had this conversation because, after all, since we believe these things *you* don't have to.

But where Cabala's interlinked meanings are said to gradually lead the devotee to a beatific vision of God illuminating everything, the twisted trails of conspiracy theory end in much darker revelations, though Illuminati may be involved. And this grimmer vision, sadly, seems considerably more in tune with the world we now find ourselves inhabiting.

Occult Nation

yself, the woman to whom I am husband, and others of our tribe just spent Monday evening impersonating dead people, drinking alcohol to the point of inebriation and dancing to exhaustion. There were devils and wizards in our midst, and at least one of us appeared to be possessed by demons. In other words, we celebrated Halloween, one of the few holidays that doesn't even try to disguise its pagan origins. It seems we will never outgrow the need to placate our ancestors, and All Hallow's Eve will always be with us.

Nor is Halloween the only pagan holiday that persists in our time. The date of Christmas and most of the customs associated with it have nothing at all to do with Christ or the Bible and are instead derived from Winter Solstice rituals that predate history. Groundhog Day is a contemporary echo of Imbolc, May Day and the maypole keep the ancient tradition of Beltane alive and did you know the very name 'Easter' is derived from the Teutonic Earth Goddess Ostara?

And of course it's not just holidays, and it's not just good old-fashioned paganism. Here in the United States, our dollar bill is emblazoned with a pyramid topped with the Eye of Horus, a magick symbol that can be traced to Dynastic Egypt, our military headquarters is housed in a version of the pentagram, and our current president is a member of the initiatory ritual magick order known as Skull and Bones and so is his father, the former president, and so was the democratic candidate in the 2004 presidential campaign - but at least the Bonesmen are a break from the usual Presidential magick society, Freemasonry. Our elite males gather yearly at the notorious Bohemian Grove to worship Molech and our

National Capitol is laid out around a reconstructed Egyptian obelisk that projects male power with the same blunt symbolism as a church steeple. And I could go on, and on and *on* and on, and if you catch me at happy hour no doubt I will, but for now let us move on to something like a point:

There is simply no escaping it; we are a superstitious people obsessed with the occult. But we certainly *try* to escape it. We burden our holidays with tacky Biblical symbolism, we accept the reflexive debunkings of the official media, and we slather on meaningless official explanations to help us deny what our own lying eyes are telling us. And that's enough for most of us, most of the time.

But as I can tell you from personal experience, being one of those people for whom it's *not* enough can be a drag - there are so many strange things that are undeniably true that it is hard not to think that some of the *really* strange things are probably also true. And once you go down that particular rabbit hole your world becomes a different place, and a scarier one.

And here is the truth that we all dance around; if the world really is overlaid with occult trappings, as it certainly is, then we can be pretty sure that they're not just trappings. Where there's smoke there's fire, and sometimes where there's fire there are burnt offerings. *We* may not believe in magick, but some of those in power clearly *do* and have felt that way for a long time... so you know what *I've* been thinking? Maybe *I* should give it a try.

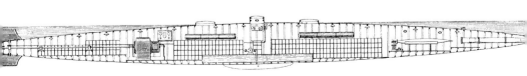

It probably seems perverse, or at least forced, to tie together the ancient and noble art of idolatry with the modern excesses of music industry executives. But nearly all political, religious, and business controversies come down to one basic dynamic - some people trying to control other people. And this is one way of getting at that fundamental issue.

Idolatry

Why does idolatry get such a bad rap? It's condemned, famously, in the second of the ten commandments but even as the commandment was being inscribed the Israelites and the Golden Calf were making a mockery of it. And idolatry never went away. The Old Testament is full of it; idolatry is vigorously condemned throughout but is never erased entirely. Grove worship and household gods prove as difficult to kill as kudzu, and as readily resurgent. And this conflict between popular desire and institutional authority isn't confined to Judaism - it's a philosophical issue in Christianity, Islam, and other religions. What is it about idol worship that so infuriates *some* humans, and why is it so attractive that a lot of *other* humans keep returning to it millennium after millennium?

The whole thing reminds me of the contemporary conflict between music industry executives and music end users. There is a vibrant culture of music downloaders and remixers and some of this is of course illegal. But in response, industry executives appear to have literally gone insane - over the past couple of years they have tried to get laws passed that would allow them to investigate every computer connected to the Internet without notification, they've tried to cripple even legitimate CD copying, and they continue to ruin lives by suing small time downloaders. Their attitude seems to be that no one is going to mess around with music without their permission. Similarly, the conflicts between established religion and 'remixed' religion have fairly often escalated into the insanity of witch hunts and genocide.

Could it be that priests - the executives of institutional religion - have control issues? That the real problem with idolatry is that it cuts out the middlemen?

Maybe, but why do humans keep coming back to idolatry despite opposition? Again, the music industry gives some insight: people keep downloading and remixing music because it's easy and fun, and sometimes the results are excellent. Idolatry has a similar appeal. Dancing in the groves sounds like a good night out and having an image of God in the house can be very comforting. Put another way, whatever it is that religion provides, idolatry also provides, without the tedium of church or the interference of priests.

There is also the possibility that idolatry works; that directly supplicating gods through images is an effective way to bring about positive change. This might offend a different set of priests, the rationalists of Science, but are several billion humans necessarily wrong?

None of this is to say that institutionalized religion is a bad thing, or that priests don't serve a purpose. Hey, if that's your trip, happy trails.

But maybe it's *not* your trip. Maybe you like to roll your own when it comes to religion and when it comes right down to it, there's no one alive who's ever been dead, which means *all of us* are making it up as we go along.

It really seems - to me anyway - that there are *at least* two kinds of people when it comes to expressing spirituality: those who like to supplicate God in a formal way with all the trappings of an established church, and those who prefer a more free-form, do-it-yourself approach. It would be nice if they could just leave each other alone.

Prayer

When I was an overzealous Christian, one of the mysteries that most stoked my fanaticism was the undeniable truth that many of my prayers were, in fact, answered and often with uncanny precision. Therefore I, like others in my preferred variant of the Jesus cult, assumed that these answered prayers were evidence of divine favor, proof that we alone were franchisees of the one True Brand.

Later in life, as I painfully matured, I noticed that *other* divisions of Christianity *also* had their tales of answered prayer, and that their experiences sounded much like mine... and might even be true. Later still, as I began to resemble a grownup in many ways, I finally accepted that even worshippers in non-Christian religions even - gasp! - atheists and heathens, also had their tales of answered prayer and other synchronicities.

Eventually, Christianity and I separated due to irreconcilable differences, but I was still interested in influencing the unseen via some 'prayer-like' technology because, after all, it beats work. So I began to investigate various techniques that had previously been anathema to me. I dabbled in ceremonial magick, for example, with remarkable results but, alas, the robes and rituals were fully as tedious as conventional religion and I gave it up.

I've also tried visualization, affirmation, written requests, channeled material, paganism and, oh, lots of other things besides... I have striven to be a well rounded heathen. And the one lesson I've learned in all my dabbling - or research, if you will - is that I'd better be careful what I ask for because I'm quite likely to get it, no matter *how* I do the asking. That is, in my experience, *everything* works; the Universe appears to be a wish granting machine that makes few, if any, judgments about the asker or about how the asking is done.

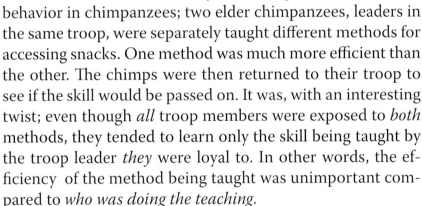

My point, and for a change I have one, is that effectiveness is *not* proof of validity or exclusivity; in other words, you probably *do* have a direct line to the divine, but you're *not* the only one getting through - you may not even have that great a connection.

I'm reminded of a recent study of learning behavior in chimpanzees; two elder chimpanzees, leaders in the same troop, were separately taught different methods for accessing snacks. One method was much more efficient than the other. The chimps were then returned to their troop to see if the skill would be passed on. It was, with an interesting twist; even though *all* troop members were exposed to *both* methods, they tended to learn only the skill being taught by the troop leader *they* were loyal to. In other words, the efficiency of the method being taught was unimportant compared to *who was doing the teaching*.

A cynic like myself can't resist the obvious comparison to human practice. We all have our religions, our philosophies, our superstitions, our methodologies for supplicating the invisible... but how many of us are simply following the example of our troop leaders and blindly condemning rival methods? How many of us have actually *investigated* the wealth of available spiritual technologies?

When it comes to religion, maybe a little comparison shopping is in order.

Realities

I t is a staple of New Age belief that we all 'create our own realities'. This is, of course, a silly, unfounded and wooly-headed idea that no sensible person subscribes to, and yet... what, really, *is* 'reality'? For most of us, I think, reality is our day to day experience of life, the information delivered to us by our senses and also, naturally, our *memories* of daily experience. But both of these fundamental aspects of reality, sense and memory, are sadly subject to manipulation.

Consider a famous experiment in human perception that dates to the 1890s; Dr. George Stratton devised a pair of goggles that reversed all the images coming into his eyes, turning them upside down. And then he wore these goggles for several days, so that he was seeing the world around him upside down. The results were astounding; after about three days of seeing the world reversed, Stratton began to see things *right side up again.* In other words, the mental software that processed data coming in through the eye adapted to the new situation. Later, when Stratton took the goggles off, he saw things upside down for a few days, until his brain readjusted.

But think about this for a moment; if the brain routinely processes something as fundamental as *up and down*, and we aren't aware of it, how can we be sure that *all* of our data isn't being processed in one fashion or another? Well, in fact - and of course - all of our sense data *is* processed; *everything* we see, taste, touch, smell and hear is converted into electrochemical signals that the brain *interprets.* And the power to interpret is the power to edit, to enhance, to rearrange. We may not be aware of it, we may not like the idea, but in fact all of us are *deciding*, on some level, what the world is like, what it looks like, smells like, tastes like, feels like.

And memory is even *more* subjective. In a series of recent studies, researchers have determined that memories are amazingly fluid. You've heard, probably, that DNA evidence has begun to exonerate hundreds of American prisoners - but did you know that many of these wrongly convicted men and women *confessed* to the crime they were accused of, and *even have distinct memories of committing it*? University of Michigan researchers believe that just being interrogated is enough to implant a false memory in some individuals.

University of California researchers have discovered that it's even easier than that. They administered a survey to college students that asked detailed questions about food preferences. Then, many of the students were given 'false feedback' - okay, they were lied to -and told that they must have had a bad childhood experience with strawberry ice cream. When prompted, 40% of the deceived students came up with memories of getting sick; clear, vivid, *completely bogus* memories.

So we unconsciously process all of our sense data, our experience of the present, and we unconsciously rearrange our memories, our experience of the past - is it really so crazy, then, to suggest that we are, unconsciously at least, creating our own reality? And really, are we so sure that it's impossible to do so consciously?

Well, I am cynical, but after I wrote this I also began to be cynical about the reality of peak oil - after all, large profit-oriented corporations are skillful and tireless propagandists, and the most obvious result of all the peak oil flap is higher prices at the pump. And Kunstler is selling a lot of books...

Long Awakening

I am a cynical person, always looking on the dark side of things. Naturally, the recent talk of peaking oil production and $60 a barrel oil prices has been catnip for me and I've been gleefully speculating about the imminent doom of the industrialized way of life.

The thing is, oil production *does* appear to be peaking, or may even have peaked already. Even oil companies, even governments, admit this to be true. This doesn't mean that the world is about to run out of oil, but oil is harder to find now, and increasingly more expensive to get out of the ground. Which means that our ridiculous, automobile-based way of life is going to become increasingly untenable, cities will die, and a new dark age is about to descend.

Or does it? This scenario, called the 'Long Emergency' by James Howard Kunstler in his recent book of that title, certainly seems both dire and unavoidable, but I have been trying to overcome my natural pessimism and see the bright side. For one thing, I suggest we immediately stop calling it the 'Long Emergency' and instead call it a 'Long Awakening'. I suggest we view the data coming in about oil production as an alarm clock going off. We've been hitting the snooze button for several years, but the time is coming when we'll have to wake up, get out of bed, and make tea.

Waking up will mean acknowledging the connections between formerly cheap oil, our way of life, and global violence. Waking up will mean acknowledging our dependence on formerly cheap oil for formerly cheap food. Waking up will mean actually creating a sustainable culture rather than depending on formerly cheap oil to fund our formerly cheap fantasies.

But here's the thing about waking up: once you're finally awake, it's wonderful. For the developed world, ending oil dependence will be as invigorating as ending any addiction. Our food will be better because it will be grown without petrochemicals. Our air will be cleaner because it will no longer be choked with smog. Our water will be cleaner, our bodies will be healthier, and perhaps the world will know peace as we stop looking to other countries for vital resources.

We are human beings, the most intelligent and resourceful creatures on the planet. We've created the Taj Mahal, jet airplanes, the Internet, Ween, and bluegrass music. We're pretty awesome. True, for many decades a lot of us have depended on cheap oil extracted from our home planet to create a bizarre lifestyle that can't be sustained but even while doing so we've done wonderful things and acquired amazing scientific knowledge. Like any addict, we think we need our drug, but when we finally break our habit we'll find that life is much sunnier.

In my own life, whenever I consciously strive to be optimistic and look on the bright side, things do turn out better. As a natural pessimist this is often irritating, but I must admit it is more fun to be positive. So why not try it as a species? Rather than clinging to our addiction, rather than fighting bloody wars to keep control of our drug, why not just 'wake up' to reality and all it's infinite possibilities? We have nothing to lose but sleep.

I am, um, increasingly unconvinced by my own arguments in this essay, and by Crichton's. Still, I continue to detect an amazing amount of hot air and bad statistics in the arguments for the global warming/CO₂ hypothesis so... who knows? And, frankly, a simple thing like Truth will never convince me to pass up a juicy line like 'steaming pile of best-selling excrement'.

State of Fear

As a novel, Michael Crichton's new *State of Fear* is a steaming pile of best-selling excrement. But as non-fiction it's quite good, *and* controversial. Crichton takes the contrarian view that global warming is a non-crisis; faddish science hyped by cynical environmental groups to pump up fundraising.

Does Crichton have the intellectual chops to make such an argument? Well, in addition to being a writer known for thorough research, he is also a graduate of Harvard Medical School, a filmmaker, and a former Medical Writer of the Year. In a word, he's smart. More to the point, the argument made in State of Fear is supported by references, 2 afterwords, and an 11 page bibliography, giving the interested reader adequate information to make her own decisions.

Ultimately, and with some reservations, I found him convincing. That puts me in the same camp as Rush Limbaugh and George Bush, which I admit hurts, but now that I have read Crichton's book and browsed a couple of web sites I too am an expert on global warming and you should listen to me. In any event, State of Fear's argument is simple and strong and is based on just a few points.

First, humans know very little about weather. We certainly don't know enough to model weather with any accuracy. We *absolutely* don't know enough to make large scale policy changes based on models and have any idea what their ultimate real world effect will be.

Second, the evidence does *not* uniformly support the global warming hypothesis. Long term weather records show that some areas are cooling, and even aggregate temperature records show recent periods of global cooling as long as 30 years, even while CO2 levels have risen. Most critically, reliable temperature records go back only 150 years or so, while weather, of course, has been around somewhat longer.

Third, though there is an observable warming trend, it is less than half a degree in a century and there is no way to tell how it fits into the planet's long term trends. Nor is it possible to know how much is natural and how much is manmade. Rising CO2 levels may not be a major factor – changing land use may have a greater effect.

Fourth, it is not true that all reputable scientists believe in global warming. There are many who think it's a crock.

I said I had reservations: Crichton is deeply suspicious of the environmental movement and implies that fundraising is a bigger concern than the state of the planet. But I notice that he doesn't provide footnotes for *this* belief. And I would feel better about Crichton's conviction if the environmentalists in his book were able to defend themselves more expertly, instead of being idiotic straw men.

Even the most brilliant essay is not going to resolve this issue in a few hundred words. If you have an interest in the topic you could read *State of Fear*, or another excellent contrarian book, *The Skeptical Environmentalist* by Bjorn Lomborg. For a climate scientist's excellent response to Crichton's book, go to realclimate.org and poke around. You might find that reading about the weather is almost as much fun as talking about it.

The following essay first appeared in The American Surveyor, a trade magazine that I am very proud to write a column for. If you happen to have seen it there I'm, um, astonished and would love to hear from you.

Two Views of One Planet

The 'Peters Projection' was announced by historian Arno Peters in a 1973 speech to the United Nations - the grandiose setting must have seemed a little over the top to serious workers in the rarefied world of cartographic projection. Nevertheless, Peters struck a nerve, and his self-titled projection became very popular indeed - many groups actively lobbied for its use in schools and it was quickly adopted by several U.N agencies and the National Council of Churches for *all* uses. In 1983 the N.C.C. even published Peters' book, *The New Cartography: A New View of the World*. Peters' map remains in vogue today, being prominently featured, for example, in an episode of television's *The West Wing*.

Why all the fuss? What was it about *this* projection that made it so popular? Well, Peters (who died in 2002) was a master at combining indisputably true points with a few that *were* disputable. He maintained that the Mercator Projection, then commonly used for wall maps, badly distorted the relative areas of world land masses so that, for instance, Europe looks much bigger than it really is and Greenland appears to be roughly the same size as Africa when in fact Africa is about 14 times larger. So far, so good, but Peters went further by claiming that the Mercator Projection was inherently racist, and unfit for *any* use. He based this on the positional and spatial prominence of developed countries as shown on the Mercator Projection. He apparently believed that only 'his' map, which accurately showed land mass areas, should be used.

Actual cartographers rolled their eyes at this. To begin with, the Mercator's problems as a *wall* map were well known, but to say it had no use at all was crazy talk - it is still indispensable to navigators because straight lines drawn on the Mercator Projection are 'loxodromes', lines that show true compass bearing between two locations. In fact, it is axiomatic among cartographers that *no* projection is suited for all uses - they all have their strengths and weaknesses.

Moreover, Peters was attacking a straw man. Long before 1973 the Mercator Projection was gradually being replaced as a wall map by several projections, notably the 1963 Robinson Projection, the invention of Arthur Robinson, probably the most eminent modern cartographer.

But most damning was Peters' claim to have *invented* the 'Peters' Projection. Cartographers recognized it as being, in fact, a special instance of the Gall Projection, published in 1885 by Scottish astronomer James Gall. At best, Peters may have independently re-invented it, and the projection is now more properly known as the Gall-Peters Projection.

For all these reasons, Arno Peters was never going to be popular with cartographers, but aside from that tempest in a teapot, the Gall-Peters Projection still has problems judged strictly on its merits. Though it does allot *area* accurately, it does so at the expense of *shape*. Toward the poles, land masses are distorted East-West but near the equator they are distorted North-South; in Robinson's scathing phase, the resulting maps look like, "... wet, ragged long winter underwear hung out to dry on the Arctic Circle." Furthermore, other equal-area projections, such as the Albers Conic or the Lambert Azimuthal, have long been available and do a better job of managing unavoidable distortions.

There is no doubt that Arno Peters was a sincere, idealistic man devoted to the cause of fairness and equality. His other major work, the *Synchronoptic History of the World*, was an attempt to tell the story of all the world's peoples, giving equal weight to each and avoiding Eurocentrism. He was also keenly aware of the power of ideas and well-versed in the techniques of getting those ideas across - in fact, his 1945 Ph.D. dissertation at the University of Berlin was titled, *The Use of Film as a Propaganda Medium*. But he wasn't a cartographer and it may be that his genuine sense of mission and flair for promotion ended up obscuring better approaches to the worthy goal of fairly and accurately representing the world in two dimensions. Nevertheless, he deserves credit for popularizing the issue and for educating the public about the problems of conventional mapping in general and the Mercator Projection in particular.

Bucky Tries His Hand

Arno Peters wasn't the only 20th century non-cartographer visionary who ended up inventing and popularizing his own map projection - Buckminster Fuller also gave it a try. Fuller (1895-1983) patented his Dymaxion Projection in 1946, based on the simple, brilliant idea of projecting the surface of the globe onto a regular solid. The 1946 version used a cuboctahedron (8 triangular faces, 6 square faces), but by 1954 Fuller was using a slightly modified icosahedron (20 triangular faces) so that the resulting Dymaxion Map could present all the Earth's land masses without breaking them up. 'Dymaxion', incidentally, is a contraction of DYnamic MAXimum tensION and is little more than 'genius style' marketing language - Fuller applied the term to cars, houses and even to his preferred sleeping pattern.

As a mathematical feat, the Dymaxion Projection is considerably more sophisticated than the Gall-Peters Projection and consequently has a number of technical advantages.

To begin with, distortion of shape and area is minimal and, more importantly, the distortion is evenly distributed. This compares favorably to most projections, which generally distort quite a bit in some parts of the globe but relatively little elsewhere. The Gall-Peters Projection is one of the worst at this since it - somewhat ironically - distorts the shape of developed countries very little but badly deforms the undeveloped countries that Peters was trying to represent more fairly!

The Dymaxion Projection can also be unfolded in different ways for different purposes - that is, the icosahedron can be laid flat with different countries at the center. This avoids much of the almost automatic emphasis that most maps give to Europe and North America, and also avoids the tendency to think of North as 'up', thus avoiding a great deal of unconscious cultural bias. In Fuller's view it was better to think in terms of 'in' - toward the center of the Earth - and 'out' - toward the stars.

The most common method of laying out the Dymaxion Map is with the North Pole more or less at the center, and seeing the Earth this way is a revelation. The separate continents appear to be not separate at all! Rather, they look like more like one large island, somewhat fragmented by water but still essentially one mass surrounded by ocean. It's a compelling view of the world and a startling contrast to *any* rectangular wall map.

Like Peters, Fuller was a tireless promoter of his many ideas and the Dymaxion Map held a special place because of its role in what he called the 'World Game'. The game was (and is) played with the aid of a large map that dynamically displays multiple world variables. Fuller's hope was that the game would evolve into a method for global citizens to directly make responsible decisions about allocation of global resources. To that end, he even produced a basketball court sized version of the Dymaxion Map, dubbed the 'Big Map', and presented it to Congress! The World Game, alas, has so far failed to replace current methods of governance, but is still widely played.

Presently, Buckminster Fuller tends to be remembered for his invention of the geodetic dome and little else. One gets the impression that he was simply too prolific to be taken seriously - his ideas and philosophies are so numerous and so far outside the mainstream that it may take the rest of us a generation or two to catch up. But it's a shame that his unique map is not better known, and almost a crime that the relatively clumsy Gall-Peters Projection seems to have displaced it as an educational tool and wall map. All of Peters' stated goals - fairness, equality, non-bias - are better achieved by Fuller's simple, elegant and brilliant creation.

Further Reading

There are several Internet sources for information on the above topics: wikipedia.org, the free online encyclopedia has excellent information on just about every topic discussed, bfi.org is the address of the Buckminster Fuller Institute and a good start for those interested in Fuller's life and work, and odt.org sells Peters Projection maps and also has a good biography of Arno Peters.

Interviewing Christopher Alexander was absolutely the nicest door ever to open for me in my writing career. He has been one of my intellectual heroes for more than 20 years. When I first thought about writing about him I was actually a little daunted, thinking that I couldn't possibly do justice to his philosophy – and perhaps I haven't. But I decided to try and actually speak with him. I expected quite a phalanx of assistants, but instead I talked to just a couple of people, primarily his chief assistant, Maggie Moore. Everyone was very helpful, and it turned out that Chris had been thinking about land surveying in connection with some of his ongoing projects. This greased the skids considerably, and when we got around to the interview, after some email exchanges, it wasn't a one way flow of information – I had the very gratifying sense that I was able to answer a few questions for him. Apparently, even one of the finest minds on the planet finds surveying a little mysterious...

Note: Clearly, the following essays on Alexander were written for surveyors (they appeared first in The American Surveyor*) but I am vain enough to think that those who enjoy all the preceding essays will find this longer piece enjoyable as well. Besides, I have pages to fill.*

Christopher Alexander: Genius of Space

Surveyors shape the world. The decisions we make in an afternoon will resonate for generations. The boundaries we propose on paper will be written on the land with wire and stone, will be enforced by law, will govern patterns of use that might persist for centuries. And yet, we make these decisions rather casually, often by the seat of our pants. In my practice, I am often concerned with just a few factors – lot yield, road frontage, minimum area, depth-to-width ratio, and sometimes existing features that can be used as buffers. My twin masters, time and money, along with zoning laws, usually prevent deeper thinking. Still, it has often seemed to me that opportunities to do good are constantly missed, or not even recognized. I guess what I often feel is a frustration that there isn't better theoretical and practical support for deep questions about land division. That is, I think it would be great if I had the leisure and responsibility to consider the future life, health and beauty of the land I am about to divide, and some methodology for doing so that was more sophisticated than simply resolving frontage and depth-to-width ratios. If surveyors had the theoretical support, we might more often notice and take advantage of our opportunities to improve the world we are making. What is needed is a genius of space.

All my life I have worshipped genius. I have sought it out even when it is a little repugnant. The comics of Robert Crumb, for example, often make my skin crawl but are so clearly the product of a certain mad brilliance that I admire them anyway. Likewise, I don't care if the genius is *useful*; I will probably never be called on to defend a Japanese village from bandits, but I have seen Akira Kurosawa's masterpiece Seven Samurai no less than 6 times and intend to see it several more times before I die.

Happily, genius is, often enough, appealing *and* useful; the best example I know of is the iconoclastic architect Christopher Alexander. He is a genius of space, best known (at least until recently) as the principal author of *A Pattern Language,* a book of architectural theory that vigorously insists that architecture – the built world – must serve humans, must strengthen and enrich the 'life' of a place. In 1977, when *APL* was published, this was, astonishingly, a highly controversial view. Alexander, in fact, became involved in a seven year long first amendment case with the University of California, which tried to prevent him teaching the material. Students who took his work seriously were often penalized by other teachers. Alexander and his supporters were heretics in the dysfunctional church of architecture. Alexander himself was not just a 'bad boy' of architecture; in many circles he was a pariah... and, in some circles, a pariah he remains.

In retrospect, it's easy enough to see why. Alexander was the little boy pointing out the non-existence of the Emperor's clothes, except in this case he was pointing out that most of the big new buildings being hailed as masterpieces really sucked for the people that had to live and work in them and that, more often than not, new buildings were destroying beautiful old cities and neighborhoods. His observations were as irritating as they were undeniable, and those who promoted, designed and built the monsters reacted vituperatively.

But Alexander wasn't out to reform architecture – that was just a side effect. He was really attempting to deal with an obvious and frustrating problem – it is really, really hard to build something wonderful, something with life. Houses, for example, should be a solved problem by now. For centuries, or for millennia, actually, humans have been not only making houses but thinking about them, codifying their modes (and modifying their codes) of construction, publishing plans, assembling not just houses but knowledge *about* houses. And yet still, after all this effort, new houses, more often than not, are kind of lousy. One exists in them, is sheltered, but one does not actually live well. We've all been in houses with no comfortable corner to read a book, no gathering places for friends to casually chat, no incentive, really, to *be* in the house. The house functions as a place to sleep, bathe, and refuel, but has no structural support for anything more intensely human. In subtle ways it fails, and will never be a home, merely a padded box with plumbing.

But when a house works, it's glorious. One walks in and instantly feels 'at home', more oneself, more alive. And the reasons for this success are not obvious. It is not related directly to expense – small huts occasionally have more life than the mansionettes so often built today. Nor is it a matter solely of location – many beautiful sites are nearly ruined by the wrong house being built on them. And I believe it can be definitely said by now that it is not a matter of having the right plan – the overabundance of housing plans has not noticeably increased the world's quantity of excellent houses. So what does make a building come alive?

Alexander first publicly explored these important questions in two books which have fascinated and infuriated architects and urban planners (among others) ever since. The first was *The Timeless Way of Building* and the second was the aforementioned *A Pattern Language. Timeless Way* is more a book of philosophy or even mysticism than a book of architectural theory – in my view it can be considered a worthy descendent of the Tao te Ching. *APL*, by contrast, is nuts-and-bolts practical; it balances Timeless Way's apparently subjective philosophy with a sort of DIY empiricism that begins by describing the proper form of world government and ends with the admonition to decorate with "things from your life." Along the way instructions are provided for, among other things, making and firing of paving stones, positioning a window seat, and constructing concrete arches.

If I make the book sound a bit of a hodgepodge, I suppose it is. It's heavily illustrated throughout with black and white photos of middling quality and extremely rough sketches. It's organized eccentrically, with each 'pattern' linked to others; actually, now that I think about it, the book (decades before the Internet) is organized much like a website except that the links, of course, are not clickable. Like a website, *APL* is easier to browse than to read sequentially. It is, in fact, compulsively browseable, the kind of book to which one happily loses hours. I sometimes thought of it as the world's most important book. Why?

Patterns seemed (and still seem) important to me because

they can be *recognized.* They take a subject as large and amorphous as 'space' – you know, that stuff we all live in - and give us a way to talk about it usefully. Alexander and his coauthors made a serious attempt to identify space that worked, that had 'life', and then to identify the underlying factors that worked for and against that space. The resulting patterns present a sort of algorithm for successfully creating similar spaces, spaces that live, and the 253 patterns are meant to be combined in ways that create rich symphonies of structure.

This sounds hopelessly dry and academic, but in fact the patterns, and the underlying concept of a language of such patterns, are so immediately apprehensible that they bypassed architects almost entirely and began to be used by lay people and contractors and that segment of the counterculture represented by *Mother Earth News* and *The Whole Earth Catalog.* Once one has read, for example, a statement as simple as,

> *"When they have a choice, people will always gravitate to those rooms which have light on two sides, and leave the rooms which are lit only from one side unused and empty."*

one is not likely to forget it, or fail to use it, and *APL* is chockfull of similarly useful verities. To many readers, *APL* was a revelation, an apparent way out of the madness that much of the built world seems to have become.

But… that was then, and this is now.

Moving On

Christopher Alexander is one of those prodigiously capable men who are as well-versed in practice as they are in theory, able to move from whole system big pictures to the grittiest details of building production. Unusually for a prominent architect, he is also a practicing general contractor. His book

The Production of Houses, for example, moves easily from the topic of large scale house production to the way plastered walls are prepared for painting.

Naturally then, all his ideas are regularly field tested and he has completed about 200 projects on 4 continents, ranging from third world housing projects to major universities. And what he's learned in the nearly three decades since *Timeless Way* and *APL* isn't totally comforting. Though the books are valid, something was missing; it was discouragingly rare for the principles to be applied by others in ways that created the sort of living space that Alexander envisioned... and without that, there was nothing.

His response was to look deeper into the nature of order itself, to try and divine the deepest possible principles underlying the kinds of space that he feels have 'life' (a word with precise and special meaning for him). Ultimately he wrote a 4 volume *magnum opus*, now being released, grandly titled *The Nature of Order*. Like Stephen Wolfram's roughly contemporaneous *A New Kind of Science*, it attempts nothing less than a fundamental reordering of humanity's worldview and, also like *A New Kind of Science*, it is reaping more than its share of both scorn and reverence. I have read Volumes One and Two, and will be reviewing them in a future column... for now, suffice it to say that I lean toward the reverent camp.

Going Further

I don't argue here that Christopher Alexander's beliefs should be adopted wholesale by the surveying community. But I do find it astonishing that they are not more widely known and discussed among surveyors. His books have had enormous influence in recent years in fields as diverse as computer programming, business organization, urban planning, and oriental carpet studies. New Urbanism borrows from Alexander.

But of all professions, save possibly architecture, surveying is the most natural and important for *actual implementation* of his program for creating a more whole and living man-made world. I, for one, would like to see it happen.

Curious readers can immediately learn more by going to www.patternlanguage.com or www.natureoforder.com, or – even better in my view – reading *Timeless Way* or A *Pattern Language*. Even though Alexander has moved on, I still believe them to be the best introduction to his thought. And then, by all means, tackle *Nature of Order*. They are difficult, mind-expanding (and rather expensive) books and even the most skeptical reader will find much food for thought.

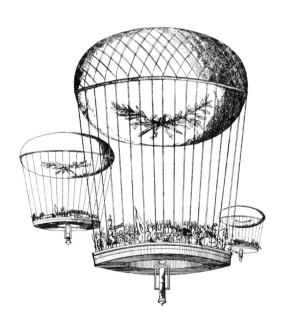

Life, the Nature of Order, and Everything

In the previous essay, I briefly profiled architect Christopher Alexander and alluded to his current project, the four book *Nature of Order*. In this essay, I'll be reviewing the first two books of the set, *The Phenomenon of Life* (TPoL) and *The Process of Creating Life* (PoCL). The prominence of the word life highlights the importance of this concept in Alexander's thinking. For him, life is a quality inherent in all things, not solely a property of plants and animals. This is not a particularly radical belief. It's a tenet of Buddhism and Taoism, and is beginning to find adherents among some scientists. The thing is, it's hard to define life in a way that *includes* creatures like animals and insects, but *excludes* things like crystals or complex computer programs. Viruses are a good example of the difficulty; are they intricate crystals that self replicate in certain animals, or are they living beings in their own right? Ask a biologist sometime, and see what he says.

In any event, Alexander defines life very broadly, and believes that it exists in the world around us in varying degrees. So, right away, we find that he is tackling some big questions: What is Life? What is Space? What is the Nature of Order? These are questions that occupy mystics, and there are some who see Alexander that way. I don't. He is too practical and hardworking, and he is not too concerned with *individual* spirituality; his focus is on reforming the built environment but, yes, he addresses… spirit.

I wish I could talk about Christopher Alexander without

getting into questions about the meaning of life, but it's no use; the man continually and infuriatingly *will* point out the 600 pound gorilla in the room that we're all trying to ignore – humans are spiritual beings, and the world is a spiritual place. We make demands on our buildings that aren't satisfied by profit and efficiency. That we so successfully avoid this reality so much of the time explains much, Alexander contends, about the often unsatisfactory nature of the world we've made for ourselves.

Spirit is always threatening to disrupt our lives; seen in a certain light, the bureaucratization of our society's large institutions seems designed to prevent such troubling eruptions – see Kafka, Charlie Chaplin, Michael Moore, et al. It is axiomatic that no priest wants a saint in his parish, but then, neither does the mayor, or the factory owner.

Alexander points out that structure, too, can work against human wholeness and spirituality and this seems logical enough. After all, no one leaves nature to get 'back to the city' when seeking peace and enlightenment. There are, of course, exceptions. Beautiful gardens or soaring cathedrals can be engines of transcendence. But these are exceptions that prove the rule; generally speaking, the built environment is perceived to repress human wholeness. Why? Why don't humans create beautiful living structure as readily as do bees, clouds, trees, or termites?

Nature of Order is a work of great detail, precision and force that attempts to answer this question. That the question of Spirit comes up, implicitly but insistently, is the work's strength and weakness. The force of *Nature of Order* is derived from Alexander's fearless exploration of the structure of the world, and the proper place of humans in that structure. But it also makes his philosophy threatening... a lot of people just want to build a better house, not wrestle with questions about the ontological grain of the universe.

Alexander's confidence can resemble hubris; and sometimes he seems to rely overmuch on intuition when making his points. To read his books well, one must surrender to them. Not abjectly, and not forever, but a certain suspension of skepticism, while reading, helps enormously when trying to absorb the material.

The Phenomenon of Life

In *The Phenomenon of Life*, Alexander gives his fullest and deepest explanation of his conception of life, and why it is more deeply felt in some places and things than in others.

Early in *TPoL*, Alexander describes an incident from his teaching career that succinctly captures many of the themes of his work, and the reasons his ideas meet resistance. He asks his students to compare two things: a picture of a 7th century illuminated manuscript (the Durham Gospel fragment) and the wall of the very auditorium in which the lecture was being held. Then he asked a simple question – which of the two had more life?

The question met enormous resistance. Not because it was hard – nearly every student agreed, albeit reluctantly, that the graceful, calm-yet-intricate manuscript held more life than the postmodern, brass-detailed wall. The *question itself* created resistance. Just admitting that one artifact can have more life than another was disturbing. If it is *possible* to enhance the life of a building, then it is *important* to do so; but the question of life is not being addressed in today's architectural curricula – except by Alexander.

Alexander finds this ability in humans consistently, and he also finds that resistance is common. When asked, people agree with amazing uniformity on the relative amount of life imbued in various objects. Although the question seems strange, *it has an answer*. But this is astonishing, because it tends to destroy the difference between the subjective and the objective. Science stoutly rejects data which cannot be measured. Human opinions, notoriously squishy, cannot be measured by any known instrument… but what if humans, in aggregate, *are themselves* effective measuring instruments?

There is another, deeper, reason for resistance. Lurking beneath Alexander's simple question is a much thornier question: if humans respond to the life of a place, and if life can be detected and worked with rather simply, how is it that so much of the built world works against life? Suddenly, the work of a developer or a surveyor moves beyond the question of profit, and into the realm of religion. Faced with this, it is much easier to fight against the question, and the person raising it. But this is denial.

Alexander makes his case for pervasive life thoroughly and with great cumulative force. He begins by discussing what he calls centers:

> *"In using the word center in this way, I am not referring at all to a point center like a center of gravity. I use the word center to identify an organized zone of space – that is to say, a distinct set of points in space, which, because of its organization, because of its internal coherence, and because of its relation to its context, exhibits centeredness, forms a local zone of relative centeredness with respect to the other parts of space. When I use the word center, I am always referring to a physical set, a distinct physical system, which occupies a certain volume in space, and has a special marked coherence."* (TPoL, p. 84)

Redefining a word as basic as 'center' – or 'life' – seems willfully inscrutable at first, but the idea is actually quite useful. Consider a pond in a clearing; it is not exactly a whole in itself, because it is part of a larger whole, the clearing, which is in turn part of a forest, and so forth. But the pond is *something*, and calling it a center does help us to see it as a locus of interest in the midst of a larger whole, a locus that *influences* that larger whole. And the idea is delightfully recursive; the clearing is itself one of many centers in the larger forest and influences that whole, which in turn is one center of a larger regional whole, and so forth.

Like Alexander's earlier concept of a pattern language (see previous essay) the value of the concept lies in its use. Learning to analyze wholes in terms of centers makes it easier to actually *see* how a whole is formed, and how it can be strengthened or how it is being weakened. It gives those who are trying to analyze space an effective analytical tool.

If it seems presumptuous of Alexander to redefine a word for his own use and to propose an entirely new way of analyzing the world, well, that is a valid criticism but it is also pretty much the point of *TPoL*. Alexander is proposing a new way of perceiving and analyzing space – he is proposing the basis for a new theory of the world's geometric underpinnings. Whether he succeeds or not is for each reader to decide.

Living wholes, then, are made up of strong centers, and the life of a whole is increased by strengthening and increasing its centers. As I began to get comfortable with this idea, I indeed found it to be a useful way of looking at the world around me, a way to figure out why I like some places more than others. *TPoL* is copiously illustrated, and the illustrations do help to convey what Alexander is getting at. But ultimately, an interested reader will have to decide for himself how useful the idea is.

Alexander continues his argument by explaining why some centers have more life than others. And here, I think, he presents an idea that is extremely compelling and immediately useful. It amounts to a general theory of aesthetics, and will likely be adopted rather quickly in the field of visual arts.

Alexander proposes that there are 15 fundamental properties – structural features – that appear consistently in things which have life. Let's just list them:

1) Levels of Scale
2) Strong Centers

3) Boundaries

4) Alternating Repetition

5) Positive Space

6) Good Shape

7) Local Symmetries

8) Deep Interlock and Ambiguity

9) Contrast

10) Gradients

11) Roughness

12) Echoes

13) The Void

14) Simplicity and Inner Calm

15) Not-Separateness

About a third of *TPoL* is devoted to a masterful exposition of this idea. The 15 properties are shown and discussed in manmade artifacts and in natural phenomena. The illustrations and text work together and gather force like Ravel's *Boléro*, culminating in an essay titled *A New View of Nature*. Ultimately we realize that Alexander has done an amazing thing; he has made it possible to talk, really talk, about why we like some things and places better than others. Rather than falling back on vapid words like 'pretty' or 'awesome' we can speak with precision about the qualities that distinguish Yosemite Valley from, say, a gravel quarry, or why we are more moved by a giant sequoia than by a mall. His beliefs and accompanying language legitimize human feeling, validate our intuitive sense of value, and, without hubris or solipsism, make the world personal.

I have barely skipped a stone over the surface of this remarkable book. In 476 exhaustively illustrated and footnoted pages, Alexander rigorously makes the case for his new view of the world, and takes initial steps toward a mathematical statement of that view. It is an intellectual tour-de-force and fully supported by his real world work as a builder and architect. The man's ideas should be taken seriously.

The Process of Creating Life

Defining life is a good start for Alexander, but the major theme of his career has been actually getting more life into modern buildings. And to do this, Alexander found, more than a definition is needed; the *what* of creation is pointless without the *how*. That is, a living building cannot be designed, then built. The life of a building comes from decisions made during the construction process. Design and construction turn out to be pretty much the same thing.

Alexander begins to talk about this by returning to one of *Nature of Order's* fundamental questions: why is it that natural processes *automatically* create beauty and a feeling of rightness, and human methods so rarely do? What is the difference?

In a series of fascinating examples ranging from a wave breaking to a glass plate shattering to a fetus developing, Alexander shows convincingly that development processes in nature are a series of structure-preserving transformations. Each recognizable phase of development follows naturally from the preceding phase. Put another way, each phase of development preserves and extends the wholeness of the preceding phase – the wholeness is never destroyed, it unfolds into a new wholeness.

Consider Edgerton's famous photos of a splashing milk drop. Though discrete phases of the sequence are startlingly different from each other, the changes from moment to moment are gentle and comprehensible. Alexander argues convincingly that this is a feature of *all* natural development.

Furthermore, the structure-preserving transformations can be analyzed in terms of the 15 fundamental properties introduced in *TPoL*. As extended here, the 15 properties become 15 transformations. Change that preserves wholeness is shown to be a product of transformation based on one or more of the 15 properties. Each transformation introduces, preserves, or strengthens one or more of the 15 fundamental properties. Again, one of the most useful things Alexander has done here is to provide good language, which makes good analysis possible.

He goes on to argue, with multiple examples, that humans *can* build in this structure-preserving fashion, but usually don't. To do this, he juxtaposes traditional (or pre-modern) building processes with modern examples. He is getting at something deep here; humans love old places. We visit New England, or Europe, to see the *old* buildings, not the modern ones. We have a sense that the old cathedrals, the old city layouts, are somehow richer. Alexander contends that traditional building methods followed the structure-preserving process he finds in nature. For example, he presents a series of plans that show the development of Amsterdam from 1400 to 1800. It is easy to see how the steady development process took previous development into account. Patterns that were latent in 1400 are realized in 1800, building shapes echo each other, the relationship of the town to the water is consistent throughout. There is no sense of planned development – Amsterdam seems to have *grown*.

The structure-preserving process occurs in the modern world, but more rarely. Beginning about 1900, many forces – changes in banking, in zoning, in planning, in architecture, etc. – began to produce *structure-destroying* transformations. The wholeness of an existing structure was no longer considered. A classic example would be the extension of a freeway through an existing neighborhood. The freeway is designed and built without reference to its surroundings, and thereby destroys those surroundings. And similar examples can be cited ad infinitum: a skyscraper designed on one continent and built on another, a planned community laid out with equal precision on the drawing board and on the ground, a giant Wal-Mart box seemingly dropped from the sky onto its scraped pad... in every case, the previously existing whole is disregarded and destroyed.

Alexander uses these examples to define two kinds of structure: generated and fabricated. Generated structure creates life, and fabricated structure, nearly always, creates... the opposite of life.

The discussion of generated structure begins with an analogy that struck me very powerfully. Consider a fairly complex origami construction. It is not built to a plan; that is, blueprints of the finished structure are not provided. Instead, a *sequence of steps* is provided. A plan of the figure would be quite complex – several pages at least. But a sequence – first do that, then do this – is relatively concise. This idea is then applied to the development of an embryo. DNA does not store a blueprint of the exact appearance of a particular animal, it stores a sequence of development which then takes place affected by attendant circumstances. Interestingly, this is proved by recent experiments in biology – cloned animals do not look exactly alike. Same sequence, different circumstances.

Brutally compressed into a nutshell, Alexander's program for creating living structure is to generate a construction sequence that first, observes the whole, then, makes a change that preserves and enhances the whole while approaching the desired end state, then... repeats as needed. Or, in his more elegant language:

> "*A living process is any adaptive process which generates living structure, step by step, through structure-preserving transformations.*"

These sequences can also be called patterns, harking back to Alexander's early book, *A Pattern Language*. Here, they emerge as part of a comprehensive program for reforming human construction methods. As argued, the case for reform is convincing and ultimately hopeful. After all, the remaining remnants of traditionally built structure are good evidence that humans *can* build in a living fashion. As a species we have been unconsciously competent, are now unconsciously incompetent, but are beginning to notice deficiencies – to be consciously incompetent. It certainly seems possible that the human capacity for self-observation must eventually lead to conscious competence, and to a beautiful living world.

PoCL is a massive book, totaling 635 pages with appendices and notes. The illustrations are copious and superbly complement arguments put forth. I have, therefore, presented barely a skeletal outline of the book's full force, but I hope I have adequately suggested that it is forceful.

In some ways, Alexander is the living human I most admire. He has, after all, come by his ideas the old-fashioned way... he's earned them. He has poured his life into his writing and philosophizing and then he has done something harder. He has, for decades, tested his philosophy, often in difficult conditions in the poorest regions of the planet. He is, simultaneously, an idealistic ivory tower dreamer and a pragmatic contractor; that dirt under his nails is a mix of grit and ink and it's been there for decades. When a man so rigorously tests his ideas in the real world, over such a span of time, and then adjusts his ideas to accord with the practical knowledge gained... well, he deserves a hearing.

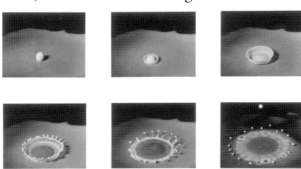

Colophon

This book was typeset with Adobe InDesign CS2 on a Mac. This wouldn't ordinarily require any comment, but since I set my previous book, Everything is Somewhere, with Microsoft Word on a Dell I feel compelled to note how incredibly nicer an experience it has been. Viva Mac!

Most of the text is set in Warnock Pro, about which I know nothing except that it's damn fine looking. The drop caps are taken from a variety of freeware fonts - that Internet, it's going places.

The 'illustrations' are Victorian era engravings of transportation, collected in a CD from Agile Rabbit Press. They are gratuitous surrealism and may be ignored.